THE IMAGE
OF OLDER ADULTS
IN THE MEDIA

THE IMAGE
OF OLDER ADULTS
—————IN THE MEDIA——————

AN ANNOTATED BIBLIOGRAPHY

Frank Nuessel

P
94.5
.A38
N84x
1992
west

Bibliographies and Indexes in Gerontology, Number 18
Erdman B. Palmore, Series Adviser

GREENWOOD PRESS
WESTPORT, CONNECTICUT • LONDON

Library of Congress Cataloging-in-Publication Data

Nuessel, Frank H.
   The image of older adults in the media : an annotated bibliography
/ Frank Nuessel.
      p.   cm.—(Bibliographies and indexes in gerontology, ISSN
0743-7560 ; no. 18)
   Includes index.
   ISBN 0-313-28018-5 (alk. paper)
   1. Aged in mass media—Bibliography.   I. Title.   II. Series.
Z5633.A39N84   1992
[P94.5.A38]
   305.26—dc20   92-24259

British Library Cataloguing in Publication Data is available.

Library of Congress Catalog Card Number: 92-24259
ISBN: 0-313-28018-5
ISSN: 0743-7560

First published in 1992

Greenwood Press, 88 Post Road West, Westport, CT 06881
An imprint of Greenwood Publishing Group, Inc.

Printed in the United States of America

The paper used in this book complies with the
Permanent Paper Standard issued by the National
Information Standards Organization (Z39.48-1984).

10 9 8 7 6 5 4 3 2 1

For

Rita E. Nuessel

CONTENTS

SERIES FOREWORD

The annotated bibliographies in this series provide answers to the fundamental question, "What is known?" Their purpose is simple, yet profound: to provide comprehensive reviews and references for the work done in various fields of gerontology. They are based on the fact that it is no longer possible for anyone to comprehend the vast body of research and writing in even one sub-specialty without years of work.

This fact has become true only in recent years. When I was an undergraduate (Class of '52) I think no one at Duke had even heard of gerontology. Almost no one in the world was identified as a gerontologist. Now there are over 6,000 professional members of the Gerontological Society of America. When I was an undergraduate there were no courses in gerontology. Now there are thousands of courses offered by most major (and many minor) colleges and universities. When I was an undergraduate there was only one gerontological journal (the *Journal of Gerontology*, begun in 1945). Now there are over forty professional journals and several dozen books in gerontology published each year.

The reasons for this dramatic growth are well known: the dramatic increase in numbers of aged, the shift from family to public responsibility for the security and care of the elderly, the recognition of aging as a "social problem," and the growth of science in general. It is less well known that this explosive growth in knowledge has developed the need for new solutions to the old problem of comprehending and "keeping up" with a field of knowledge. The old indexes and library card catalogues have become increasingly inadequate for the job. On-line computer indexes and abstracts are one solution, but they make no evaluative selections nor organize sources logically as is done here. These annotated bibliographies are also more widely available than on-line computer indexes.

These bibliographies will obviously be useful for students and researchers who need to know what research has (or has not) been done in their field. The annotations contain enough information so that the researcher usually does not have to search out the original articles. In the past, the "review of literature" has often been haphazard and was rarely comprehensive, because of the large investment of time (and money) that would be required by a truly comprehensive review. Now, using these bibliographies, researchers can be more confident that they are not missing important previous research; they can be more confident that they are not duplicating past efforts and "reinventing the wheel." It may well become standard and expected practice for researchers to consult such bibliographies, even before they start their research.

The research and writing relevant to aging and the media has become a large and rapidly growing field. This is attested to by the 558 references in this bibliography and by the wide variety of disciplines represented here. Thus this volume will be useful to professionals and researchers in many different fields.

The author has done an outstanding job of covering all the recent literature and organizing it into an easily accessible form. Not only are the references organized into 21 topical chapters, but there is also an introduction, an author index, and a subject index with many cross-references.

Thus, one can look for relevant material in this volume in several ways: (1) look up a given subject in the subject index; (2) look up a given author in the author index; or (3) turn to the chapter that covers the topic.

Dr. Nuessel is exceptionally well qualified to prepare this bibliography. He is Professor of Modern Languages and Linguistics at the University of Louisville and has published several articles on related subjects (see the author index).

So it is with great pleasure that we add this bibliography to our series. We believe you will find this volume to be the most useful, comprehensive, and easily accessible reference work in its field. I will appreciate any comments you care to send me.

Erdman B. Palmore
Center for the Study of Aging and Human Development
Box 3003, Duke University Medical Center
Durham, NC 27710

PREFACE

Two decades ago, a reference manual such as this one would have been both impossible and unthinkable. In the first instance, the extant research would not have justified such an undertaking, hence its impossibility. In the second instance, the notion that an annotated bibliography devoted to the topic of the image of an older adult would be worthy of an entire book would have been just as incredible. Nevertheless, the past twenty years have seen a veritable explosion of interest in, and research on topics related to aging with the result that specialized reference works such as this one have become a necessary resource.

There are 558 references included in this volume. Some of the categories contain only a few entries, while other areas feature abundant citations. In this sense, this reference book points out areas for future study. Moreover, many of the areas of scholarly study covered in this volume require further investigation, or followup studies to determine their current status.

This volume is divided thematically into 21 chapters. The citations are listed alphabetically by author, and chronologically in the case of multiple references. Each citation has a chapter number followed by its numerical entries in a chapter. The Author Index and the Subject Index feature this same format (chapter number followed by numerical position in the chapter) to facilitate precise location of the materials in the text proper.

I would like to acknowledge the assistance of Erdman B. Palmore, series editor, and George F. Butler, editor, behavioral and social sciences, Greenwood

Press. Their significant support in the preparation and development of this bibliographic reference was noteworthy.

I would also like to thank Sandy García for the preparation of this manuscript. Without her customary patience, understanding, and excellent work this project could never have been completed.

INTRODUCTION

It is perhaps wise to discuss briefly two of the terms employed in the title of the present resource work to avoid referential confusion. These words are "older," or more precisely, the base form "old," and "media."

A satisfactory definition of the term "old" remains elusive. In essence, this attributive adjective is a social construct derived from developmental psychology. "Old" only has significance as a reference point along a continuum of longevity. In this century, for example, the life expectancy for a citizen of this country has increased from 47 to 75 years. In that sense, the reference point for a purely chronological notion of "old" has changed.

An abundant literature exists on the multi-disciplinary dimensions of this notion of "old" (Erikson, 1959; Holmes, 1983; Keith, 1982; Levinson, 1978). The crudest basis for labeling a person old is to refer to the number of years lived, that is, a strictly chronological dimension. Discussions of the multi-dimensional nature of aging are common. Age-grading in different societies is accomplished in a number of ways (Holmes, 1983, pp. 23-35; Keith, 1982, pp. 16-34).

Holmes (1983, p. 27) has noted that "regardless of how the life cycle is divided, all societies recognize old age as a definitive status." Criteria for the determination of this final portion of the life cycle are divergent. The least revealing approach, yet the most frequently used, is a gross chronological measurement of number of years lived. This version of old age is often employed in the United States even though it fails to take into account important factors such as personality, vitality, biological condition, psychological state, and mental ability (Holmes, 1983, p. 27). An alternative method of determining "oldness" is the functional approach. In this view, old age occurs when a person "is no longer able to be a fully productive, participating member of society" (Holmes, 1983, p. 27). The latter version of old age may be considered a biased approach because this kind of research views "oldness" in negative terms and assumes that "the characteristics of the aged not only have something to do with the difficulties of aging but that they in fact cause them" (Levin and Levin, 1980, p. 3).

The frequently used term 'media' requires some discussion because of the frequent imprecision in its usage. In this reference work, the word refers to both the print and non-print manifestations of communication. The print media include traditional verbal formats such as books, newspapers, magazines, and other printed formats which are primarily logocentric in their presentation. In today's increasingly technological world, much of what we read is projected onto the video display units of computers located in the home, work place, and various libraries. These computers, in turn, access various data bases.

The non-print media are generally considered to refer to television, radio broadcasts, recordings (vinyl records, compact discs, tape cassettes), video-cassettes, artistic creations (painting, sculpture, film, photographs), and computer games. In fact, non-verbal communication (paralanguage, kinesics, proxemics) is an inherent feature of most non-print media. To a certain extent, however, much of the non-print media derives from printed or scripted materials. Most of what we see on television, film, and in dramatic presentations, or even what we hear on recordings or broadcast on radio derives from the printed word. It is perhaps only the representational arts such as music and visual art that lack a verbal basis. Therefore, in speaking of the image of the older adult in the media, the reference is often to an admixture of verbal and non-verbal, print and non-print manifestations.

INTERDISCIPLINARY NATURE OF AGING STUDIES

By its very nature, the study of aging is an interdisciplinary pursuit. The phenomenon of growing old entails biological, chemical, physiological, psychological, and social dimensions. In addition, reflection on the significance of aging involves profound philosophical, and ethical questions. Many creative people (writers, artists, thespians) have interpreted its meaning during the past several millennia, thereby providing a wider audience with some comprehension of the multi-faceted nature of aging. It is perhaps this aspect of aging in gerontological studies that renders the field so interesting, and challenging.

RELATED BIBLIOGRAPHIES

A number of bibliographies have appeared that relate tangentially to the present one. Nevertheless, there is virtually no overlap in content or category. The bibliographic resources included in this section complement the present reference work by providing the reader with easy access to related areas of scholarship.

AGEISM

Prejudice and discrimination on the basis of age are practices that have existed for far longer than the term that has ultimately labelled this form of bias. It was Robert N. Butler (1969) who coined the neologism for this convention a quarter of a century ago. In that essay, the concept was defined in the following way: "age-ism reflects a deep seated uneasiness on the part of the young and middle-aged--a personal revulsion to and distaste for growing old, disease, disability; and fear of powerlessness, 'uselessness,' and death" (p. 243).

Butler reinforced this negative vision of age-based prejudice and discrimination in his Pulitzer Prize-winning book Why survive?: Being old in America (p. 12) by quoting a description of this phenomenon from his earlier collaborative book on aging and mental health (Butler and Lewis, 1973):

> Ageism can be seen as a process of systematic stereotyping of and discrimination against people because they are old, just as racism and sexism accomplish this with skin color and gender. Old people are categorized as senile, rigid in thought and manner, old-fashioned in morality and skills. . . . Ageism allows the younger generation to see older people as different from themselves; thus they subtly cease to identify with their elders as human beings.

The traditional connotation of ageism has been one of negative reference, that is, that this practice is harmful and pernicious to older people. Levin and Levin (1980) devoted an entire book to this topic. The idea of a uniformly negative treatment of older adults has not been without its detractors.

It would not be, however, until Palmore (1990) that a more balanced perspective would be presented. In his recent book on this subject, Palmore (1990, p. 4) defined ageism as "any prejudice or discrimination against or in favor of an age group" [emphasis in original, FN].

ATTITUDES AND STEREOTYPES

An attitude, simply stated, is a state of mind or disposition toward some matter. In the context of this reference, attitude refers to the set of beliefs that a person has about a particular group of people, in this instance, older adults. These attitudes may be negative or positive. The culture and the environment in which a person lives shapes that individual's attitudes and perspectives. Therefore, the cultural artifacts may contribute to perceptions about members of our society. Symbolic manifestations manufactured by the various institutions of a society, therefore, are quite powerful tools in the creation of ideologies that permeate a given society. The print and non-print media are cultural institutions that reflect, or even create reality.

The great American journalist Walter Lippmann wrote about the notion of stereotypes in his important book Public Opinion (Lippmann, 1922). In that volume, Lippmann (1922, p. 22) referred to stereotypes, both negative and positive, as pictures in our heads. By this phrase, Lippmann meant that stereotypes allow people to categorize, and recall information more easily. Recent research in cognitive linguistics confirms this earlier assertion (Lakoff, 1987).

According to Keith (1982, p. 12), five dimensions of age differentiation exist, namely; cognitive, ideological, normative, social, and corporate. The cognitive dimension of age as a social boundary refers to "its use as a principle of categorization" (Keith, 1982, p. 13). The normative-ideological alludes to a group of "individuals who recognize that they share some characteristic, or who realize that others perceive them as sharing it, may develop a sense of collectivity of shared fate, norms about how they should behave, and beliefs about how others should treat them" (Keith, 1982, p. 13). The social or interactional dimension of age differentiation involves the kinds of interactions that occurs among age-mates (Keith 1982, p. 14). Finally, age corporations, groups formed solely by reference to chronological age, may play a significant role in age homogeneity (Keith 1982, p. 14).

Keith (1982, p. 25) notes that two basic forms of social classification exist. On the one hand, there are ascribed characteristics (race, kinship, or age), and achieved characteristics (occupation, education). The former are immutable while the latter are subject to individual control.

COMMUNICATION

Communication is a term that admits various meanings. On the one hand, this word refers to a discipline in which various aspects of micro-communication (interpersonal relations), and macro-communication (organizations, the mass media). At the level of the individual, communication alludes to vocal determinants in age identification, speech disfluencies, and so forth (Coupland, Coupland, and Giles, 1991). While a person's style of communication is revealing, other people's perceptions of another individual's speech often reflects deep-seated stereotypes and attitudes (Stewart and Ryan, 1982).

MEDIA GUIDELINES

Several sets of voluntary guidelines exist to guide authors and creative artists in providing a neutral, non-ageist depiction of older adults, for example, the American Association of Retired Persons' Truth about aging (Gamse, 1984). Circulation, and distribution of such materials serve to make the public aware of certain institutionalized, subconscious ageist practices that might otherwise go unnoticed. Careful judgment must always be exercised in the usage of guidelines, however, in order not to infringe upon the constitutionally-guaranteed principle of free speech.

LITERATURE

Creative literary characterizations depict older adults in a variety of ways. These range from literature targeted at the juvenile and adolescent market to the artistic masterpieces of established, and critically-acclaimed authors. The latter category often reflects societal attitudes of a particular epoch, while the former may, in fact, contribute to current ageist attitudes prevalent in U.S. society.

In recent years, North American academic institutions have begun to offer courses that deal with humanistic perspectives on aging. One response to this has been the publication of an annotated bibliography of the treatment of old age in the various literary genres (Yahnke and Eastman, 1990). That resource, in conjunction with the annotated entries on literary criticism and the literature of aging contained in this volume, will be useful for the scholarly community.

ART

The graphic depiction of aging enjoys a long tradition. Covey (1991), for example, has chronicled various aspects of aging conveyed in art. Among the specific elements treated are the "ages of life" theme, older people and the family, sexuality, and death. In this same fashion, McKee and Kauppinen (1987) examine the following themes of aging: (1) old age in art; (2) different ways of aging; (3) the wisdom of old age; (4) generations; and (5) the representation of old age in myths.

HUMOR

The subject of a society's humor often reveals much about its collective fears, psychoses, and preoccupations. Humor allows a culture to deal with a subject that is perceived as frightful by treatment of that topic in a somewhat detached way. In this domain, various studies on oral humor (jokes, stories, tales), and printed versions of humor about aging (greeting cards, cartoons, joke books) have appeared. This research indicates the specific domains (Palmore, 1971; Sheppard, 1981; Demos and Jache, 1981) of humor which provide some insights into current popular concerns about aging. Knowledge about these preoccupations offers an opportunity to educate the public about these matters (Palmore, 1988, 1990).

NEWSPAPERS AND MAGAZINES

Newspapers, and magazines are among the most commonplace examples of the print media. Treatment of older adults in, and by these media forms has often been stereotypic. More often than not, however, the older person is excluded. Studies exist on such specific topics as advice columns (Gaitz and Scott, 1975), advertising (Gantz, Gartenber, and Rainbow, 1980), as well as content analyses of particular newspapers (Buchholtz and Bynum, 1982) and magazines (Kent and Shaw, 1980). Though small in number, these research projects are indicative of the recent situation in these media formats.

HISTORY

The inclusion of history in the depiction of older adults is particularly important in any consideration of the image of the older adult in the media. To a certain extent, the attitudes about older people and aging today derive from past trends and historical circumstances. One approach to an explanation of the shift in attitudes toward older adults and old age results from the somewhat imprecisely defined notion of "modernization" theory (Achenbaum and Stearns, 1978), or the idea that as societies become more modern, a drop in the status of its older population occurs (Holmes, 1983, p. 167).

FILM

The cinematographic depiction of older adults includes several noteworthy examples, for example, "Harry and Tonto," "Cocoon," and many others. Yet systematic examination of these popular representations of aging is sporadic. Study of film depiction of older adults is a fertile area of research in the future.

MUSIC

The verbal content of music is largely scripted. As a result, this medium straddles the print and non-print domain. Content analysis of popular music reveals a depiction of old age which is often unflattering, and frequently ageist (Cohen and Kruschwitz, 1990; Kelley, 1982).

ORAL HISTORY

Recording the recollections and reminiscences of older adults is a burgeoning area of interest facilitated by high technology (cam-corders, tape recorders). On occasion, this form of personal remembrance has been raised to an artistic level (Blythe, 1979). Moreover, manuals now exist to assist in carrying out oral history projects properly (Thompson, 1978). Likewise, the "life review," a therapeutic aspect of reminiscence, has been discussed in the well-known treatise of Robert Butler (1963).

TELEVISION

A half century ago, television was a novelty. During the past 50 years, however, television has become a permanent fixture in our daily routine, and for some, an obsession. Because of television's unremitting intrusion into our lives, its influence is constant. This popular medium is at once a cause, and a cure of the erroneous perceptions of older adults and old age in late twentieth century North America. Because of television's inherent ability to influence attitudes, study of the depiction of older adults in this medium is especially important. Research (Davis and Davis, 1985) reveals, however, that while the characterization of aging and older people on television programming is negative, this situation can be changed.

FUTURE RESEARCH

A substantial amount of research that sheds light on the image of older adults in the media already exists as evidenced by the studies cited in this reference work. Several of the essays reflect work carried out a decade or more ago. Replication of certain of these studies would be worthwhile to determine if any essential shifts (positive or negative) have occurred in the intervening years. Moreover, fundamental changes in the delivery of the media (video cassette recorders, compact discs, cable television, computers and computer informational services) all represent the rapid transformation in media technology--a trend that will only accelerate in the remainder of this century.

FORMAT AND ARRANGEMENT

The entries correspond to the format prescribed in Publication Manual of the American Psychological Association (American Psychological Association 1984, pp. 118-133).

The annotated entries in this research bibliography are arranged into 21 categories. Each category forms a numerically-sequenced chapter, for example, "Related Bibliographies" is the first chapter. Within this first chapter, each entry contains the chapter number followed by a hyphen and the number of the particular citation in the following fashion: 1-1, 1-2, 1-3, and so forth.

The "Author Index" contains the author's surname followed by the initials of the given name(s), for example, Smith, J. and the chapter, and numerical reference within the chapter. Thus, the following entry in the author index Wood, V., 3-31, 10-8 may be interpreted to mean that work by this author appears in chapter 3, entry number 31, and chapter 10, entry number 8. In the case of sequential entries by a single author, the following format is used: Palmore, E. B., 3-70--3-77. This means that the references to Palmore include items 70 through 77 in chapter 3.

The "Subject Index," likewise, conforms to the format employed in the Author Index, that is, after each category there is a chapter reference followed by the specific entry within the chapter.

CONCLUDING REMARKS

The various popular media formats noted in this introduction demonstrate the pervasive nature of its print and non-print formats which permeates our consciousness. To some extent, this ecological saturation affects perceptions and creates stereotypic images of the extremely heterogeneous population grouped under the collective label "old." In certain cases, the boundary lines between print and non-print media have become blurred. This volume provides an account of how older people are depicted in the media, and, as a result, an insight into how contemporary society views old age. The image of aging at this point in time is mixed. Although both positive and negative features exist, research shows that many of the depictions of aging, and old age are negative. This volume chronicles the present situation, and will provide information on sources of the extant research to the interested reader.

REFERENCES

Achenbaum, W. A., & Stearns, P. N. (1978). Essay: Old age and modernization. The Gerontologist, 18, 307-312.

American Psychological Association. (1984). Publication manual of the American Psychological Association. 3rd ed. Washington, DC: American Psychological Association.

Blythe, R. (1979). The view from winter: Reflections on old age. New York:Harcourt, Brace, Jovanovich.

Buchholtz, M., & Bynum, J. (1982). Newspaper presentation of America's aged: A content analysis of image and role. The Gerontologist, 22, 83-88.

Butler, R. N. (1963). The life review: An interpretation of reminiscence in old age. Psychiatry, 26, 65-76.

Butler, R. N. (1969). Age-ism: Another form of bigotry. The Gerontologist,9, 243-246.

Butler, R. N. (1975). Why survive? Being old in America. New York: Harper Torchbooks, Harper & Row Publishers.

Butler, R. N., & Lewis, M. I. (1973). Aging and mental health: Positive psychological approaches. St. Louis, MO: C. V. Mosby.

Cohen, E. S., & Kruschwitz, A. L. (1990). Old age in America represented in nineteenth and twentieth century popular sheet music. The Gerontologist, 30, 345-354.

Coupland, N., Coupland, J., & Giles, H. (1991). Language, society, and the elderly. Oxford: Blackwell.

Covey, H. C. (1991). Images of older people in Western art and society. New York: Praeger.

Davis, R. H., & Davis, J. A. (1985). TV's image of the elderly: A practical guide for change. Lexington, MA: Lexington Books.

Demos, V., & Jache, A. (1981). When you care enough: An analysis of attitudes toward aging in humorous birthday cards. The Gerontologist, 21, 209-215.

Erikson, E. H. (1959). Identity and the life cycle. Vol 1, no. 1. New York: International Universities Press.

Gaitz, C. M., & Scott, J. (1975). Analysis of letters to "Dear Abby" concerning old age. The Gerontologist, 24, 415-419.

Gamse, D. N. (1984). The truth about aging: Guidelines for accurate communications. Washington, DC: American Association of Retired Persons.

Gantz, W., Gartenber, H. M., & Rainbow, C. K. (1980). Approaching invisibility: The portrayal of the elderly in magazine advertisements. Journal of Gerontology, 30, 56-60.

Holmes, L. D. (1983). Other cultures, elder years: An introduction to cultural gerontology. Minneapolis, MN: Burgess Publishing Company.

Keith, J. (1982). Old people as people: Social and cultural influences on aging and old age. Boston: Little, Brown, and Company.

Kelley, C. E. (1982). Ageism in popular song: A rhetorical analysis of American popular song lyrics, 1964-1973 (Doctoral dissertation, University of Oregon, 1982).

Kent, K. E. M., & Shaw, P. (1980). Age in Time: A study of stereotyping. The Gerontologist, 20, 598-601.

Lakoff, G. (1987). Women, fire, and dangerous things: What categories reveal about the mind. Chicago: University of Chicago Press.

Levin, J., & Levin, W. C. (1980). Ageism: Prejudice and discrimination against the elderly. Belmont, CA: Wadsworth Publishing Company.

Levinson, D. J. (1978). The Seasons of a Man's Life. New York: Ballantine Books.

Lippmann, W. (1922). Public opinion. New York: Penguin Books.

McKee, P. L., & Kauppinen, H. (1987). A celebration of old age in Western art. New York: Human Sciences Press.

Palmore, E. B. (1971). Attitudes toward aging shown by humor. The Gerontologist, 11, 181-186.

Palmore, E. B. (1988). The Facts on Aging Quiz: A handbook of uses and results. New York: Springer Publishing Company.

Palmore, E. B. (1990). Ageism: Negative and positive. New York: Springer Publishing Company.

Sheppard, A. (1981). Response to cartoons and attitudes toward aging. Journal of Gerontology, 36, 122-126.

Stewart, M. A., & Ryan, E. B. (1982). Attitudes toward younger and older adult speakers: Effects of varying speech rates. Journal of Language and Social Psychology, 1, 91-109.

Thompson, P. (1978). The voice of the past: Oral history. 2nd ed. Oxford: Oxford University Press.

Yahnke, R. E., & Eastman, R. M. (1990). Aging in literature: A reader's guide. Chicago: American Library Association.

1

RELATED
BIBLIOGRAPHIES

1-1. Allyn, M. V. (1979). <u>About aging: A catalog of films with a special section on cassettes</u>. Los Angeles, CA: Ethyl Percy Andrus Gerontology Center University of Southern California.

This excellent resource tool contains 3 sections: (1) 16 mm films; (2) video-cassettes; and (3) feature length films. Each annotated entry contains information on the producer, its availability and the distributor. A second section features 40 separate categories together with the title of each film. A final section includes an alphabetical list of each distributor with address and telephone number.

1-2. Balkema, J. (1986). <u>The creative spirit: An annotated bibliography of the humanities, arts and aging</u>. Washington, DC: National Council on Aging.

This reference work contains citations in the following major categories: general aging; community organization and services; the economics of aging; housing, institutional care; health; mental health; recreation, and education. A name index and a subject index complement this work.

1-3. Borenstein, A. (1982). <u>Older women in 20th-century America: A selected annotated bibliography</u>. New York and London: Garland Publishing Company.

In its 17 chapters, Borenstein provides citations in the following domains: Activism against ageism and social criticism; autobiographies; creativity and productivity in later life; cross-cultural perspectives on aging; gerontology; housing and living environments; life-span development; literature and aging; middle age; novels and novellas by and about older women; oral histories; personal documents of older women; psychological perspectives on aging; short stories by and about women; social and economic issues; sociological perspectives on older women; and selected bibliographies. This work contains a name index. 885 items.

1-4. Coyle, J. M. (1989). Women and aging: A selected, annotated bibliography. New York: Greenwood Press.

The focus of the entries selected for inclusion in this volume is the period 1980-1988. Specific areas covered include: Roles and relationships; economics; employment; retirement; health; sexuality; religion; housing; racial and ethnic groups; policy issues; international concerns; and middle age. A subject index and a name index are included. 622 entries.

1-5. Edwards, W. M., Flynn, F., Fraser, M. D., & Slater, R. (1982). Gerontology: A cross-national core list of significant works. Ann Arbor, MI: Institute of Gerontology, The University of Michigan.

This resource work features 3 parts: (1) historical perspectives; (2) reference works; and (3) subject sources. A glossary, author index and title index are included. Each of the 3 main sections is divided into pertinent subdomains to facilitate its use as a reference work.

1-6. Eyben, E. (1989). Bibliography: Old age in Greco-Roman antiquity and early Christianity: An annotated select bibliography. In T. M. Falkner & J. de Luce (Eds.), Old age in Greek and Latin literature (pp. 230-251). Albany, NY: State University of New York Press.

Among the areas of aging included in this selective bibliographic essay are: (1) old age as a part of the life span; (2) general overviews; (3) specific studies; (4) early Christianity; and (5) other aspects. A list of references is appended (pp. 242-251).

1-7. Freeman, J. T. (1979). Aging: Its history and literature. New York: Human Sciences Press.

This reference is an invaluable bibliographical account of the history, literature and documentation of gerontology. Its 4 chapters feature: (1) a history of gerocomy from the ancient to the modern period; (2) 100 distinguished works on the topic; (3) a classified bibliography (1900-1975); and (4) a classified list of journals (to 1975). A Subject Index (156-159) and a Name Index (159-161) complement this work.

1-8.   Harris, D. K.   (1985).   The sociology of aging: An annotated bibliography and sourcebook. New York: Garland Publishing, Inc.

The 8 parts of this bibliographic reference work deal with the following themes: (1) introductory materials; (2) culture and society; (3) social inequality; (4) social institutions; (5) environment and aging; (6) periodical literature; (7) resource materials on aging; and (8) offices, associations, and centers on aging. A helpful index is included.

1-9. Hollenshead, C., Katz, C., & Ingersoll, B. (1977). Past sixty: The older woman in film and print. Ann Arbor, MI: Institute of Gerontology, The University of Michigan--Wayne State University.

Social and psychological issues, the role in marriage and the extended family, widowhood, health, sexuality, legal and economic issues, ethnic background, humanities, film and videotape are the 8 thematic subdivisions for the 283 entries contained in this annotated bibliography.

1-10. Horner, C. T. (1982). The aging adult in children's books & nonprint media. Metuchen, NJ: The Scarecrow Press, Inc.

Divided into 2 subsections, the first (Annotated Bibliography, pp. 3-191) contains 337 annotated entries for 3 categories: preschool and primary grades; intermediate grades; and middle school and high school. The second section (Multimedia section, pp. 195-242) features separate, unenumerated, annotated sections (filmstrips and slides, game and simulation, magazine articles, motion pictures and videotapes, records/cassettes/audiotapes, resource materials, and textbooks and non-fiction books). A useful introduction (pp. vii-xxiii) provides useful background materials from empirical studies in children's literature. See 1-17.

1-11. Kastenbaum, R. (1991). Review of Where do we come from? What are we? Where are we going? An annotated bibliography of aging and the humanities by D. Pollisar, L. Wygant, T. Cole, & C. Perdomo. Washington, DC: Gerontological Society of America. International Journal of Aging and Human Development, 33, 247-248.

This is a brief, and positive review of this GSA-sponsored project. Kastenbaum provides a few tantalizing hints at the content of this reference work. See 1-18.

1-12. Monroe, M. E., & Rubin, R. J. (1983). The challenge of aging: A bibliography. Littleton, CO: Libraries Unlimited, Inc.

The 5 sections of this reference book treat the following general themes: (1) aging as opportunity; (2) tasks of adjustment; (3) tasks of major change; and (4) tasks of opportunity. An author-title index and a subject index are included.

1-13. Moody, H. R. (1984). A bibliography on reminiscence and life review. In M. Kaminbsky (Ed.), The uses of reminiscence: New ways of working with older adults (pp. 231-236). New York: Haworth Press.

This useful enumerative bibliography is divided into books and dissertations, and articles.

1-14. Moody, H. R., & Cole, T. R. (1986). Aging and meaning: A bibliographic essay. In T. R. Cole, & S. A. Gadow (Eds.), What does it mean to grow old? Reflections from the humanities (pp. 247-253). Durham, NC: Duke University Press.

Although brief in scope, Moody and Cole succeed in enumerating the significant works related to the humanities and aging. This essay is divided into the following thematic divisions--the life cycle, modernity, death, and time. Disciplinary perspectives (philosophy, psychology, religion, arts and literature, history, anthropology, sociology) are also noted.

1-15. Moss, W. G. (1976). Humanistic perspectives on aging: An annotated bibliography and essay. Ann Arbor, MI: Institute of Gerontology.

This reference contains a selective, annotated listing of literary works that deal with the theme of aging.

1-16. Murguía, E., Schultz, T. M., Markides, K. S., & Janson, P. (1984). Ethnicity and aging: A bibliography. San Antonio, TX: Trinity University Press.

The 7 chapters in this bibliographic reference treat the following general themes: (1) Multiethnic and general studies; (2) Black Americans; (3) Hispanic Americans; (4) Native Americans; (5) Asian and Pacific Americans; (6) European origin ethnic groups; (7) other bibliographies. 1,432 items.

1-17. Oppenheim-Golub, M. (1983). Review of The aging adult in children's books and nonprint media: An annotated bibliography by C. T. Horner, Metuchen, NJ: The Scarecrow Press. The Gerontologist, 23, 219-220.

Though brief, the reviewer recommends this book as an essential tool in assessing the effect of the depiction of the older adult in juvenile literature on children's attitudes toward that group. See 1-10.

1-18. Polisar, D., Wyggant, L., Cole, T., & Perdomo, C. (1988). Where do we come from? What are we? Where are we going?: An annotated bibliography of aging and the humanities. Washington, DC: The Gerontological Society of America.

This monographic annotated resource contains 1099 entries with 6 sections (ethics and philosophy, history, literature and art, religion, jurisprudence, and interdisciplinary humanities) plus an author index and subject index. See 1-11.

1-19. Richardson, B. E. (1969 [1933]). Old age among the Greeks. New York: AMS Press.

Literature, art, and inscriptions form the data-base for this account of old age in ancient Greece. A Concordance and Index to Literature (237-243), a Concordance and Index to Art (244-276), and a Catalogue of Inscriptions (277-360) are important resource materials. This reference contains 27 photographs of artwork.

1-20. Yahnke, R. E., & Eastman, R. M. (1990). Aging in Literature. Washington, DC: Association for Gerontology in Higher Education.

This "brief bibliography" is designed "to help anyone who wishes to explore the usefulness of literature in illuminating the aging process" (p. 1). Its 10 pages have a selected listing of educational materials, anthologies, and literary resources on aging.

1-21. Yahnke, R. E., & Eastman, R. M. (1990). Aging in literature: A reader's guide. Chicago: American Library Association.

The compilers employ a genre approach (novels, stories, plays, poems, nonfiction) for the 517 entries in this annotated reference. 2 appendices (Aging in Literature: Major Life Responses, and Aging in Literature: Anthologies) plus author and topical indices contribute to this volume's usefulness.

2

AGEISM

2-1. Barbato, C. A., & Feezel, J. D. (1987). The language of aging in different groups. The Gerontologist, 27, 527-531.

A sample of 54 people each from 3 distinct age groups (17-44, 45-64, and 65+) in a three-state region (Ohio, West Virginia, Michigan) were surveyed to determine participant reaction to 10 nouns commonly employed to refer to older adults. Results of the survey indicate that preferences were comparable across 3 age groups, with the single exception that the youngest group favored the term "mature American" over "senior citizen." Research results showed that 3 terms were preferred ("senior citizen," "mature American," and "retired person"). This study indicates that further research on terminology is necessary to ascertain linguistic preferences and to assist gerontologists in the utilization of language that is sensitive to this age category.

2-2. Barrow, G. M., & Smith, P. A. (1979). Aging, ageism, and society. St. Paul, MN: West Publishing Company.

The central focus of this book is ageism in U. S. society. Each chapter focuses on various issues and problems faced by older adults including sexuality, health, family and friends, work and leisure, economics, living environments, and death and dying. Particular issues are considered, i.e., victimization of older people, the special situation of minority old, aging in other cultures, and the emergence of "senior" power. Photographs and cartoons that relate to each issue are also included. A chapter-by-chapter list of suggested readings, discussion questions, as well as a subject index and an author index complement this work.

2-3. Binstock, R. H. (1983). The aged as scapegoat. The Gerontologist, 23, 136-143.

Several ageist stereotypes have prevailed in public discussions. Until 1978, older adults were perceived as poor, frail, powerless, and a part of the "deserving poor." Since 1978, however, these stereotypes have been reversed. The revised view sees older adults as economically comfortable and politically powerful.   Moreover, due to changing demographics, this segment of our society will present a financial drain on the rest of society. These new axioms have facilitated the scapegoating of older adults. The effect of this practice is to divert attention from failure in leadership and public policy. The author offers specific ways to address the problems of older people without victimization.

2-4. Bunzel, J. H. (1972). Note on the history of a concept--gerontophobia. The Gerontologist, 12(part 1), 116, 203.

In this letter to the journal editor, Bunzel notes that the term gerontophobia refers to an irrational fear and loathing of older adults by members of society or by older people themselves. Proof that this malady is an actual psychological affliction requires further empirical verification.   The author chides his colleagues to study this phenomenon further. See 2-37.

2-5. Bunzel, J. H. (1973). Recognition, relevance and deactivation of gerontophobia: Theoretical essay. Journal of the American Geriatrics Society, 22, 77-80.

Gerontophobia, or the irrational hatred of older adults, may be treated through 3 basic procedures: (1) mass education; (2) insight therapy; and (3) intra-group mobilization.

2-6. Butler, R. N. (1969). Age-ism: Another form of bigotry. The Gerontologist, 9, 243-246.

In this now classic essay, Butler created the neologism "ageism" which has become a part of our basic vocabulary. Although the practice of discrimination against older adults on the basis of age existed long before this behavior received a name, its genesis as a lexical item may be traced to Butler. The author discusses various manifestations of this form of prejudice.

2-7. Butler, R. N. (1975). Why survive?: Being old in America. New York: Harper & Row.

This Pulitzer-prize winning book remains a valuable reference work. Even though the statistical data cited in this study are dated, many of the trends and issues continue to be pertinent. Among the many issues analyzed in this book are ageism, involuntary retirement, housing, victimization of older adults, health care issues, economic problems, suicide and death. The 5 appendices (Sources of Gerontological and Geriatric Literature, Organizations Pertaining to the Elderly, Government Programs for the Elderly, Government Agencies for the Elderly, and Other National Organizations with Programs in the Field of Aging) merit updating in a revised edition given the voluminous output of research in this burgeoning field. See 2-20.

2-8. Butler, R. N. (1980). Ageism: A foreword. Journal of Social Issues, 36(2), 8-11.

Ageism has 3 manifestations: (1) prejudicial attitudes; (2) discriminatory practices; and (3) institutional policies and practices. Butler notes that this form of bigotry continues to be viable and virulent in U. S. society.

2-9. Butler, R. N., Lewis, M. I., & Sunderland, T. (1991). Aging and mental health: Positive psychosocial and biomedical approaches. 4th ed. New York: Merrill.

This book is a thorough discussion on the topic of mental health and old age prepared by 3 outstanding professionals in the field. The current factual information provided in this book is indispensable for distinguishing truth from myth in this area. Popular beliefs about the mental well-being of older adults is notoriously distorted. A balanced picture on this multi-faceted area with special attention to problems of ageism is offered.

2-10. Cohen, E. S. (1988). On the Covey article. The Gerontologist, 28, 708.

The former editor of The Gerontologist praises an article by Covey (see 2-14).

2-11. Cohen, E. S. (1989). Cohen replies. The Gerontologist, 29, 709.

In this response to a letter to the editor by Schonfield (see 2-42), Cohen disputes certain comments. Cohen notes that ageism pervades our society even if some fail to recognize this form of discrimination and prejudice.

2-12. Comfort, A. (1967). On gerontophobia. <u>Medical Opinion and Review</u>, <u>3</u>(9), 30-31, 33, 37.

Dislike of older adults by some physicians presents a special problem in their treatment. Sources of this "gerontophobia" include that fact that older people will die, thereby, deflating the putative omnipotence of the doctor and the discipline of medicine to help people become better physically. Moreover, the physician must face his or her own mortality. Since the treatment of older people may be affected by such attitudes, it is important to include a humanistic educational component in our medical schools.

2-13. Comfort, A. (1976). Age prejudice in America. <u>Social Policy</u>, <u>7</u>, 3-8.

While aging has a physical component to it (certain maladies associated with senescence), there is a second sociogenic component which is disturbing. According to the author, the general public appears to have a more negative image of older adults than do older people of themselves. This pervasive ageism derives from institutional practices such as mandatory retirement which results in an "enforced idleness." Comfort argues for a continuing, useful and functional role for older adults in this society. This attitudinal transformation will require education and perseverance.

2-14. Covey, H. C. (1988). Historical terminology used to represent older people. <u>The Gerontologist</u>, <u>28</u>, 291-297.

In this historical study of terminology employed to designate older adults, Covey surveyed dictionaries such as the <u>Oxford English Dictionary</u> as well as other sources. The author seeks to determine semantic shifts in the meaning of the lexicon related to older adults over time. Several key terms are reviewed ("old," "eld," "senility"). Words that refer to older men are more favorable than those that allude to older women. In his conclusion, Covey asserts that the transformation in attitudes toward older people is reflected in the shifts of meaning of the vocabulary which refers to this group. See 2-10, 2-42.

2-15. Duncan, K. J. (1963). Modern society's attitude toward aging. <u>Geriatrics</u>, <u>18</u>, 629-635.

In this panoramic essay, several broad topics are discussed: (1) the status of older adults in a rural society; (2) emergence of aging as a social problem; (3) the effects of industrialization and urbanization; (4) reactions to aging; (5) old age as a modern issue; (6) the impact of retirement from the work force on the older adult; (7) old age as a social movement. Duncan believes that abundant opportunities exist to improve the situation of older people in this society.

2-16. Freeman, J. T. (1985). Gerontism: A neologism. Experimental Gerontology, 20, 71-72.

In this "special article," Freeman proposes a new term "gerontism" as a general word to indicate all aspects of aging. The purpose of this neologism is to create a neutral lexical item to refer to all aspects of gerontology and geriatrics.

2-17. Gatz, M., & Pearson, C. G. (1988). Ageism revised and the provision of psychological services. American Psychologist, 43, 184-188.

Professional ageism may not be as widespread as some critics would suggest. Gatz and Pearson state that treatment of older people may derive from systemic problems rather than negative attitudes. Such problems include accessibility, amount of reimbursement for services, and staff assignments. The authors, however, state that a new form of ageism has emerged, namely, the tendency to "overdiagnose" Alzheimer's disease. Appropriate education of psychologists is an effective way to deal with this emergent trend.

2-18. Gruman, G. J. (1978). Cultural origins of present-day "age-ism": The modernization of the life cycle. In S. F. Spicker, K. M. Woodward, & D. Van Tassel, Aging and the elderly: Humanistic perspectives in gerontology (pp. 359-387). Atlantic Highlands, NJ: Humanities Press.

In this excellent and informative essay, Gruman provides the historical and cultural foundation of ageism. Next, the ideological factors which underlie age prejudice and discrimination are discussed. Finally, the author challenges the theory of disengagement and proposes a model of "re-engagement" in its place.

2-19. Jensen, R. D., & Oakley, F. B. (1982). Ageism across cultures and in perspective of sociobiologic and psychodynamic theories. International Journal of Aging and Human Development, 15, 17-26.

A review of 71 pre-literate societies shows that older members retain specific roles unlike the U.S. where these functions are often lost. A sociobiological analysis explains the predominance of the pre-literate social pattern by 3 axioms: (1) stable age distribution; (2) reproductive values; and (3) a theory of inclusive fitness. Implications of this study include better education of younger people to counteract stereotypes and myths about older people. Likewise, viable roles for older people are necessary.

2-20. Kalish, R. A. (1977). Review of Why survive?: Being old in America by R. N. Butler, New York: Harper & Row. Journal of Gerontology, 32, 356-357.

Kalish finds fault with this book for its interpretation of previous research and its pervasive, negative portrayal of old age. See 2-7.

2-21. Kalish, N. (1979). The new ageism and the failure models: A polemic. The Gerontologist, 19, 398-402.

In the author's view, there exists a "new ageism" which characterizes the older adult as incapable, and helpless.   Furthermore, this new form of age discrimination and prejudice promotes the creation of services for older people without regard to the effect of such institutions on its recipients. Finally, the new ageism focuses only on the negative side of aging through a constant barrage of criticism of our society. Four prominent ageist models (Pathology Model, Decrement Model, Minimal Change Model, and Normal Person model) in this society are critiqued. Kalish proposes a new approach--The Normal Person Model: A Personal Growth Model as an alternative to the previous 4. In this approach, the older individual continues to grow and develop.

2-22.   Kearl, M. C., Moore, K., & Osberg, J. S.   (1982).   Political implications of the "new ageism." International Journal of Aging and Human Development, 15, 167-183.

Most studies of ageism have focused on the psychological aspects of the issue. More recently, however, the political dimension has begun to be explored. The purpose of this essay is to determine if aging has become a structural part of society, hence, a part of the consciousness of the individual. In this statistical analysis of data derived from Louis Harris' survey of "Myth and Reality of Aging in America," the authors have found some evidence of a new ageism, i.e., the notion that older people are an identifiable group that requires special attention. The evidence includes a trend to work together to enhance the social and economic status of older people.

2-23. Laube, C. J. (1980). Up from ageism. Media & Methods, 16, 16-18, 41.

According to Laube, ageism has 3 specific manifestations: (1) economic deprivation; (2) segregation; and (3) caricaturization. The author then provides a brief recent history of the rise of ageism in this society. To combat ageism, a reintegration of older people into society is required. This may be achieved through intergenerational programs, educational initiatives, and similar approaches. A side-bar provides facts and figures to debunk traditional myths about old age.

2-24. Levin, J., & Levin, W. C. (1980). Ageism: Prejudice and discrimination against the elderly. Belmont, CA: Wadsworth Publishing.

This work is an essential basic reference on the phenomenon of ageism. The 5 chapters treat the following topics: (1) the interdiscipline of gerontology and its focus on decline; (2) the practice of blaming the victims of ageism for their plight; (3) a thorough discussion of the concept of older adults as a minority group; (4) suggested appropriate reactions to the practice of ageism; and (5) a set of suggestions for dealing with ageist discrimination and prejudice. A thorough and useful set of references on the various topics discussed and an index complement this excellent work.

2-25. Nilsen, A. P. (1978). Old blondes just dye away: Relationships between sexism and ageism. Language Arts, 55, 175-179.

In this essay, Nilsen discusses the prevalence of ageism in this society. Although women and men are subject to ageism, it is older women who are victimized more often by age discrimination and prejudice. The author exemplifies her contentions by reference to humor and language. A set of 6 recommendations are provided to combat ageism: (1) encourage intergenerational contacts; (2) disclose your own age; (3) include information on older adults in the classroom; (4) avoid ageist textbooks; (5) integrate non-ageist readings in the curriculum; and (6) involve girls in academic pursuits, and provide positive rewards for such activities.

2-26. Nuessel, F. (1982). The language of ageism. The Gerontologist, 22, 273-276.

An examination and description of 75 words and phrases in the English language reveals an overwhelming number of pejorative terms related to aging and older adults. When applied to people, the words "aged" or "old" have a negative connotation, yet when used with objects (cheese, wood, etc.), their reference is positive. Patterns of ageism include distortion, degradation, exclusion and subordination. Since most materials for the print and non-print media derive from scripted materials, it is suggested that a plan of action for educating the public about age-based prejudice and discrimination which would include voluntary media guidelines be designed to help eliminate ageism from prepared copy.

2-27. Nuessel, F. (1984a). Ageist language. Maledicta, 8, 17-28.

A discussion of ageist terminology in the English language features specific examples of the words with an explanation of how this vocabulary functions to denigrate an entire group in our society. The few positive lexical items are also discussed. An "ageist lexicon" of 130 words with corresponding definitions is appended to this essay.

2-28. Nuessel, F. (1984b). Ageist language. The Gerontologist, 24, 334.

The author notes the existence of two sets of media guidelines designed to help avoid ageist language (see 5-4).

2-29. Nuessel, F. (1984c). Old age needs a new name: But don't look for it in Webster's. Aging, 346 (September), 4-6.

Ageist language is pervasive in our language as evidenced by the numerous derogatory terms for old age and older people. Since euphemism serves to make an unpleasant topic more attractive, the existence of euphemistic names for retirement and nursing care facilitates the isolation of the older members of our society. Suggestions for the elimination of linguistic distortions are offered.

2-30. Nuessel, F. (1986). Language and ageism. Linkages, 1(4), 5-6.

Benjamin Lee Whorf postulated that language is an instrument for shaping our concepts about our environment. If this hypothesis is true, then the English language inventory of terms that refer to old age and older adults promotes the practice of ageism. Selected exemplification of ageist language is provided and some suggestions for combating this aspect of prejudice and discrimination are provided.

2-31. Nuessel, F. (1987). On the Barbato and Feezel article. The Gerontologist, 27, 809.

In this letter to the editor, the author states that the act of naming is a symbolic gesture which means that the "namer" has power over the named group. For this reason, it is suggested that older adults select the term by which they wish to be known as an act of empowerment, self-determination, and autonomy. The author suggests the term "older adult" as a possible neutral phrase.

2-32. Nuessel, F. (1989a). Ageism and language. Aging Network News, 5(9), 4, 17, 20.

The author reviews previous research on the ageist properties of the English language. The pervasive nature of such language in our daily lives is likely to affect our attitudes toward older people. The existence of ageist language has the potential to shape the next generation's perceptions of older adults.

2-33. Nuessel, F. (1989b). Ageism and language. Linkages, 3(1), 6-7.

This is an abridged version of the previous essay (2-32).

2-34. Nuessel, F. (1991). The semiotics of ageism. International Semiotic Spectrum, 16, 1-4.

In this essay, the author discusses definitions of the life cycle and places aging in a U.S. context. A definition of ageism is then provided. The sociological notion of age as a stigma is then explored. Common manifestations of ageism in U.S. society are reviewed and exemplified. Finally, the semiotics (overt symbolism) of ageism are explored. The author shows that certain common symbols (grey hair, cane, clothing, etc.) stand for old age. Because of this society's fear of the usually negative consequences of aging, many people seek to conceal their membership in this group through a variety of subterfuges, thereby reinforcing their fear of growing old.

2-35. Nuessel, F., & Stewart, A. V. (1989). The use of popular print media visuals to dispel common negative attitudes toward older adults. In D. L. Gardner, & M. C. Hoekelman (Eds.), Developing leadership in geriatric education: Proceedings of the fourth annual summer institute (pp. 155-157). Lexington, KY: Ohio Valley Appalachia Regional Geriatric Education Center.

In this essay, the 4 mechanisms (distortion, degradation, subordination, and exclusion) of ageist prejudice and discrimination are discussed. The authors then proceed to discuss methods (selection and identification of appropriate materials, determination of presentation format, and a systematic file by themes) for employing popular printed materials as tools to dispel negative beliefs and concepts about aging and older adults.

2-36. Ossofsky, J. (1975). Viewpoint: National organization seeks to mend frayed image of the elderly. Geriatrics, 30, 42, 44, 46.

In this interview with then executive director of the National Council on the Aging, Ossofsky discusses various aspects of ageism in U.S. society (compulsory retirement, the youth-oriented educational establishment). The leader of the NCOA states that his organization is seeking to dispel erroneous beliefs about older adults.

2-37.   Palmore, E. B.   (1972).   Gerontophobia versus ageism.   The Gerontologist, 12(3, part I), 213.

In this letter to the editor, Palmore responds to Bunzel's (see 2-4) discussion of gerontophobia by noting that the latter is a rare phenomenon, while ageism is more pervasive in this society. It behooves the professional to combat the more widespread problem of ageism.

2-38.   Palmore, E. B.   (1990a).   Ageism.   Center Report [Duke University Center for the Study of Aging and Human Development and the Geriatric Education Center], 10(1), 2, 8.

In this essay, Palmore points out that the public views ageism as a negative form of discrimination. In fact, this practice may also be positive, i.e., favor older adults. A brief discussion of individual and institutional ageism ensues. Finally, the author sets forth an individual and group agenda for reducing ageism.

2-39.   Palmore, E. B.   (1990b).   Ageism: Positive and negative. New York: Springer.

This essential reference on ageism is the most comprehensive and current reference on this topic. In this work, Palmore discusses the subject of ageism as a negative and positive phenomenon in our society. The book contains 4 parts consisting of 3 or 4 chapters each. Part I ("Concepts") features 3 chapters which conceptualize, define, and classify the types of ageism. The 4 chapters of the following section ("Causes and Consequences") outline the individual, social and cultural causes of ageism. In addition, the consequences of this form of discriminatory behavior are outlined.   In the 4 chapters of Part III ("Institutional Patterns"), the institutional patterns of ageism in the economy, government, family, and housing and health care are explained and exemplified. The last part ("Reducing Ageism") contains 4 chapters about effecting individual and structural change. Moreover, a set of helpful strategies for change and Palmore's knowledgeable speculation about the future are included.   2 appendices ("Facts on Aging Quizzes" and "Ageist Humor"), derived from the author's extensive previous research on these subjects, complement this volume. An extensive set of references and a valuable index will also prove to be worthwhile. See 3-70, 3-74, 10-16, 10-17, 10-18.

2-40.   Palmore, E. B., & Manton, K. (1973). Ageism compared to racism and sexism. Journal of Gerontology, 28, 363-369.

In this empirical analysis, the authors compare the effects of patterns of inequality caused by age, race and gender. Palmore and Manton conclude that the highest correlation of age and inequality occurs in education and weeks worked. Furthermore, age inequality increases among men and non-whites as compared to women and whites. Age in combination with race and gender is an additive factor for inequality. Finally, non-whites and women have achieved small increases in their status while older adults are falling behind in education and income.

2-41. Ray, D. C., Raciti, M., & Ford, C. V. (1985). Ageism in psychiatrists: Association with gender certification and theoretical orientation. The Gerontologist, 25, 496-500.

According to the authors of this essay, many psychiatrists are reported to display negative attitudes toward older adults. These researchers re-examined data obtained from a previous study on psychiatrists' attitudes toward older adults. 3 variables (gender, eclecticism in theoretical approach, and board-certification) were examined to determine if these factors influenced attitudes. None of the hypotheses postulated by the authors was sustained, i.e., the 3 variables noted failed to have a positive impact on psychiatrists' attitudes toward their older patients. Suggestions are offered to combat ageism in the helping professions.

2-42. Schonfield, D. (1989). Language of aging or ageism? The Gerontologist, 29, 708-709.

In this letter to the editor on the article by Covey (see 2-14) and Nuessel (see 2-26), Schonfeld alludes to his own essay (see 3-85) in which he argues that ageism is not as prevalent as many researchers imply.

2-43. Sontag, S. (1972, September 23). The double standard of aging. The Saturday Review pp. 28-29, 31-38.

This well known author discusses the differentiating effects of age and aging on men and women in this society. In the United States, older men gain respect, while women lose value as they become older. This duality or "double standard" derives from socially determined characteristics assigned to "masculinity" and "femininity." Socially determined male and female differences appear most obviously in sexuality. Women lose their eligibility at a relatively young age while men maintain their attractiveness for a longer period. In fact, the very features that count against a woman (wrinkles, grey hair, etc.) serve to enhance a male since these overt markers signal maturity and wisdom. Society's attitude toward male and female aging reflects the secondary status of women in general. Sontag counsels women to liberate themselves from the superficial values assigned to them by society.

3

ATTITUDES
AND STEREOTYPES

3-1. Aaronson, B. S. (1966). Personality stereotypes of aging. Journal of Gerontology, 21, 458-462.

86 adjectives from the Gough Adjective Rating Scale were employed in this experiment to determine how two groups would describe typical person from ages 5 to 85 at ten-year intervals. An experimental and a control were tested. The results of this experiment confirm that certain stereotypes about age groups exist and may be grouped into 3 general periods: (1) childhood; (2) adulthood and (3) old age.

3-2. Arluke, A., & Levin, J. (1982). Second childhood. Public Communication Review, 1(2), 21-25.

The perception of older adults as children is pervasive in this society. Extant research confirms this hypothesis. This stereotype is perpetuated in several ways: (1) persistent pairing of older people with children; (2) assignment of children's activities to older adults; (3) clothing that is childlike; and (4) role reversals in which parents function as children of their own children. Acceptance of childlike status by older adults has negative consequences such diminution of social status, an implied permission to be treated as second-class citizens, and a devaluation of their political power base.

3-3. Arluke, A., & Levin, J. (1984, August-September). Another stereotype: Old age as a second childhood. Aging, 346, 7-11.

Stereotypic images are often culturally or institutionally fostered views of a particular group within a society. A prevalent stereotype of older adults is childlike behavior. This perception derives from the commonly held belief that older people demonstrate puerile characteristics such as dependency, disruptive conduct, and selfishness. The infantilization of older adults allows society to relegate these people to an inferior and secondary status similar to that of children. Continuation of this erroneous stereotype dehumanizes a significant segment of the population.

3-4. Auerbach, D., & Levenson, R., Jr. (1977). Second impressions: Attitude changes in college students toward the elderly. The Gerontologist, 17, 362-366.

In this study, 60 subjects (30 male, 30 female undergraduate students enrolled in a required humanities course in which older adults were enrolled) were the Kogan Old People Scales in the second and final week of the course. A control group consisted of the same number students enrolled in a psychology class. The results of this experiment showed a significant deterioration of attitudes toward older people on the second administration of the OP scale. This result indicates that there is a parallel with the case of ethnic contacts in which competition was involved. In the latter situation, resentment and rancor toward the ethnic group occurred.

3-5. Austin, D. R. (1985). Attitudes toward old age: A hierarchical study. The Gerontologist, 25, 431-434.

In this test of attitudes toward old age, Austin employed an assessment instrument based on an earlier form in which 144 students enrolled in 2 courses in the summer and fall of 1982 participated. A ranking of 21 "disabilities" included physical infirmities that included categories such as asthma, alcoholism, ex-convict, mental illness, and old age. Results indicate that older people are viewed in a relatively positive fashion by virtue of ranking in fifth position (tied with heart disease). The findings of this study support a view that attitudes toward old age are improving.

3-6. Axelrod, S., & Eisdorfer, C. (1961). Attitudes toward old people: An empirical analysis of the Tuckman-Lorge questionnaire. Journal of Gerontology, 16, 75-80.

In this study, 280 students (170 male, 107 female, 3 unidentified gender) were given the Tuckman-Lorge questionnaire on attitudes toward older adults. A fifth of the participants were randomly assigned questionnaires where the ages of the people in the vignettes were changed (35, 45, 55, 65, 75 years of age). Results showed that the stereotypic traits increased as the age specified on the testing instrument increased. This means that any test designed to measure attitudes toward older people must consider the stimulus-group validity of the items employed.

3-7. Bachelder, J. (1989). Effectiveness of a simulation activity to promote positive attitudes and perceptions of the elderly. Educational Gerontology, 15, 363-375.

Development of activities that stimulate positive attitudes toward older adults is one way of combating such stereotypes. The author reports on a simulation about sensory changes in the elderly within an experimental framework designed to change student attitudes. The method selected for this experiment is an experiential approach. 44 junior-level students enrolled in an occupational therapy program participated in this test. The experimental group developed more positive attitudes while the control group became more negative. This result contradicts previous studies that employed the same procedures, yet documented more negative attitudinal outcomes.

3-8. Bagshaw, M., & Adams, M. (1985-1986). Nursing home nurses' attitudes, empathy, and ideologic orientation. International Journal of Aging and Human Development, 22, 235-246.

A sample of 363 volunteer nursing personnel (62 registered nurses, 62 practical nurses, 239 nursing aids) from 7 different nursing homes in Cleveland, Ohio was carried out to assess correlation of the variables of empathy, attitudes, and ideologic orientation toward custodial and therapeutic treatment. Testing instruments employed were The Personal Inventory, The Kogan Old People Scale, The Gilbert and Levinson Custodial Mental Illness Scale, and the Empathy Construct Rating Scale. Results indicate major differences in empathy, negative attitudes and custodial orientation in the nursing homes studied.

3-9. Baltes, P. B., & Schaie, K. W. (1974, March). Aging and IQ: The myth of the twilight years. Psychology Today, 35-38, 40.

This overview of IQ tests, Baltes and Schaie point out that many such tests are age-biased, hence, these instruments show a decline in mental ability. IQ tests fail to distinguish between competence and performance. Thus, any use of these tests must take into account a variety of factors before it is possible to make an absolute judgment that older people have a real intellectual decline.

3-10. Barron, M. (1953). Minority group characteristics of the aged in American society. Journal of Gerontology, 8, 477-482.

Do older adults constitute a minority group? In an early examination of this question, Barron examines the attitude of the majority group (perception of the older person as a menace and acts of prejudice and discrimination) toward older people as well as the attitude of the minority group towards itself (bitterness, resentment and self-hatred). The author concludes that older people represent a quasi minority. Because members of minority groups are often victimized by the propagation of erroneous perceptions, this study is relevant to the notion of stereotype.

3-11. Bassili, J. N., & Reil, J. E. (1981). On the dominance of the old-age stereotype. Journal of Gerontology, 36, 682-688.

In an experiment involving 180 college students (mean age of 22.4) and 180 older adults (mean age of 75.6), Bassili and Reil administered a stereotype differential instrument which involved gender, occupation, race, and age. Results indicate that both groups stereotype older people primarily on the basis of their age. The stereotypical older adult is seen as being conservative, traditional, present-oriented, and moral.

3-12. Bell, B. D., & Stanfield, G. G. (1973a). The aging stereotype in experimental perspective. The Gerontologist, 13, 341-344.

In this empirical analysis of the attitudes of 280 University of Missouri college students, Bell and Stanfield played a recorded tape of a stimulus person who was portrayed as either 25 or 65 years of age. The subjects were then asked to respond to the 46-item Tuckman-Lorge Stereotype Scale. Results indicated no significant differences in the experimental or control groups. This experiment raises important questions about the use of chronological categories to assess age-based stereotypes as well as the overwhelmingly negative nature of responses reported in previous research.

3-13. Bell, B. D., & Stanfield, G. G. (1973b). Chronological age in relation to attitudinal judgments: An experimental analysis. Journal of Gerontology, 28, 491-496.

In order to determine the effect of knowledge about the chronological age on a person's attitudes, 2 experiments were carried out. The first group of subjects consisted of 280 traditional college-age students, while the second involved 96 older adults. Participants listened to a recorded conversation designated as a 25 year old or a 65 year old. This stimulus was followed by the 32-item Rosencranz and McNevin aging semantic differential questionnaire. Results indicated that there was a minor, though statistically insignificant tendency, to rate the younger person more highly.

3-14. Bengston, V. L. (1971). Inter-age perceptions and the generation gap. The Gerontologist, 11 (part 2), 85-89.

The term "generation gap" was coined 2 decades ago to describe the differences in values between younger and older adults. This essay discusses 3 parameters for intergenerational perceptions: (1) age of the person whose perceptions are being analyzed; (2) the referent group or person; and (3) the context of the bias and prejudice. 278 people (from potential 3-generation families) answered and returned the questionnaire. Results indicated that a significant gap exists between the oldest and the youngest members of a family. Replication of his study would be useful.

3-15. Blau, Z. S. (1956). Changes in status and age identification. American Sociological Review, 21, 198-203.

A sample of 468 people from Elmira, NY over the age of 60 participated in this study. Participants were asked to rate themselves as to age-group (middle-aged, elderly, or old). Results showed that 60% of the respondents considered themselves to be middle-aged. Blau sought to account for this response. Results of her inquiry revealed that retirement was the one factor that seemed to hasten the recognition of self as old because this status amounts to an official judgment of old age. Widowhood, although a traumatic experience, involves a single social interaction, and is not linked to old age per se.

3-16. Braithwaite, V. A. (1986). Old age stereotypes: Reconciling contradictions. Journal of Gerontology, 41, 353-360.

A total of 208 Canberra, Australia high school students (ages 16 to 19) participated in a study to assess stereotypes of older adults. Students engaged in 2 activities. The first involved 4 vignettes in which the main character was either 71 or 26 years of age. The participants then evaluated the person according to various traits (active and sociable, responsible, etc.). The second task involved the evaluation of generalized target. Results indicated that there are both positive and negative stereotypes about old age. Qualitative data suggest that the notion of stereotype requires more critical assessment than heretofore received.

3-17.   Braithwaite, V., Gibson, D., & Homan, J.   (1985-1986).   Age stereotyping: Are we oversimplifying the phenomenon?   International Journal of Aging and Human Development, 22, 315-325.

An experiment designed to assess the use of stereotypes of individual behavior in specific contextual situations involved 100 university students (71 females, 29 males).   Each subject evaluated 4 vignettes (younger female, older female, younger male, older male) using the Rosencranz Semantic Differential instrument.   The results indicate that global stereotypes were not involved in making assessments of an older person.   Instead, images of subgroup stereotypes of older people emerged, e.g., dependent older adult, wise older adult, and isolated older adults.   From these patterns of particular behavior, there emerged certain stereotypes.   The authors call for expanded research into age stereotyping.

3-18.   Brewer, M. B., Dull, V., & Lui, L.   (1981).   Perceptions of the elderly: Stereotypes as prototypes.   Journal of Personality and Social Psychology, 41, 656-670.

This report of 3 studies on the perception of older adults.   In 2 experiments, picture-sorting and trait-evaluation were employed.   Results indicated that categorization of older people as a social category occurred.   A third test involved Rosch's notion of category prototypicality.   In this investigation, the researchers found that retention and accuracy of recall about the category "older person" corresponded to consistency with prototypes. The authors conclude that the process of stereotyping takes place at the basic level rather than at superordinate levels.

3-19.   Brewer, M. B., & Lui, L.   (1984).   Categorization of the elderly by the elderly: Effects of perceiver's category membership.   Personality and Social Psychology Bulletin, 10, 585-595.

2 empirical investigations were replicated from an earlier study (see 3-18).   The first dealt with the categorization by younger and older subjects of two sets of photographs (one group of older and younger females and a similar set for males).   A second study set out to determine if subcategorization of older people correlated to distinctive behavioral characteristics.   Again a younger and older group of subjects participated.   Results indicated that older people demonstrated a greater degree of discrimination in the evaluation of members of the category considered to be old than did their younger counterparts.   Potential implications

of this study indicate that the majority may not distinguish differentiation among the members of the group considered to be old with the result that stereotypic perceptions may be facilitated.

3-20. Brubaker, T. H., & Powers, E. A. (1976). The stereotype of "old": A review and alternative approach. Journal of Gerontology, 31, 441-447.

This valuable overview essay reviews 47 research reports on stereotypes of old age. The results of this exhaustive research review show a discrepancy between theory and research. The authors found that positive stereotypes of old age and older adults exist. This finding indicates that older people are likely to have more positive views of old age than younger people. In addition, previous self-concept will influence the positive or negative perception of old age. Brubaker and Powers recognize the need for further research on their proposal.

3-21. Bultena, G. L., & Powers, E. A. (1978). Denial of aging: Age identification and reference group orientations. Journal of Gerontology, 33, 748-754.

A 10-year longitudinal study was undertaken to determine how people categorized themselves. In 1960, there were 611 respondents (60 years or older) to the survey. A decade later, 269 of the original group were available for reinterview, and 235 responded. In the original study, 70% considered themselves middle-aged, while in 1970 only 32% claimed this. Likewise, the percentage of people labeling themselves as "old" increased from 6% to 25%. Likewise, those who claimed to be "elderly" went from 19% to 30%. This research sustains the claim that peer reference comparisons are important for age-identity.

3-22. Cameron, P. (1972). Stereotypes about generational fun and happiness vs. self-appraised fun and happiness. The Gerontologist, 12 (2, part 1), 120-123, 190.

A survey of 317 adults representing 3 generations (young adults, middle-aged, older adults) was conducted to determine their relative happiness. Results indicated that young adults were perceived as having the most opportunities for happiness, and that middle-aged adults were the happiest, while older adults were seen as the least happy. In general, the 3 generations showed no major differences in self-reported happiness, and opportunities for happiness.

3-23. Campbell, M. E. (1971). Study of the attitudes of nursing personnel toward the geriatric patient. Nursing Research, 20, 147-151.

An evaluation of the attitudes of nursing personnel (147 subjects located in 2 teaching institutions in North Carolina) employed the Tuckman-Lorge Questionnaire. Among the results of this study are the following: (1) each category of nurse (registered nurse, licensed practical nurse, nursing assistant) showed some stereotyped attitudes; (2) registered nurses had the lowest acceptance rate of stereotypes; (3) licensed practical nurses and nursing assistants were more willing to work with geriatric patients; (4) education and time spent with older patients affected the willingness of nursing personnel to work with older patients.

3-24.   Carver, C. S., & de la Garza, N. H.   (1984).   Schema-guided information search in stereotyping of the elderly. Journal of Applied Social Psychology, 14, 69-81.

Recent psychological theories on cognition hold that stereotypic information is stored in and retrieved from memory in a schematic fashion. The experiment described in this article was designed to test the hypothesis that the evocation of one stereotype, older adults in this instance, would make the participants search for related stereotypical information. In this study, the participants read a description of an automobile accident in which the driver was either an older adult or a younger person. Results showed that when a neutral description of an older driver was the protagonist, the subjects invoked latent stereotypes about this group.

3-25. Chandler, J., Rachal, J., & Kazelskis, R. (1986). Attitudes of long-term care nursing personnel toward the elderly. The Gerontologist, 26, 551-555.

Attitudes of long-term care nursing personnel can have a significant impact on the type of treatment received by older patients. Participants in this experimental program were selected from 2 long-term care facilities on the Gulf Coast of Mississippi. The 101 subjects included 10 RNs, 21 LPNs, and 70 NAs. An experimental and a control group was established. Attitudes were measured by Palmore's Facts on Aging Quiz 1, and 2, and Kogan's Attitudes Toward Old People Scale. This program had 2 main objectives: (1) to increase awareness about attitudes toward older people; and (2) to help the participants to make some realizations about their own aging. Results indicated an unexpected degree of neutrality in nursing care staff attitudes toward older people. This situation runs counter to much of the literature on the topic and, therefore, suggests that further research is necessary.

3-26. Crockett, W. H., Press, A. N., & Osterkamp, M. (1979). The effect of deviations from stereotyped expectations upon attitudes toward older persons. Journal of Gerontology, 34, 368-374.

In this experiment, 245 male and female students read an interview with a woman who was identified as either 36 or 76. Each interviewee talked about her life, and the previous day's experiences. The participants then recorded their impressions of the woman. The older woman was depicted as engaging in stereoptypic behavior for older adults. The results showed that the older woman was perceived more favorably than the younger woman despite the stereotypic behavior pattern. Student comments indicated that an older woman who is vital and involved is interesting and deviates from the stereotypical older person.

3-27. Cyrus-Lutz, C., Gaitz, C. M. (1972). Psychiatrist's attitudes toward the aged and aging. The Gerontologist, 12, 163-167.

In this study, a sentence completion format was employed to determine attitudes of mental health care professionals toward their older patients. Questionnaires mailed to 435 psychiatrists yielded 175 responses. Responses to this survey indicated that the most frequent negative responses to the older client were boredom, impatience, and resentment of the physical deterioration of the aged. Although more research is called for, this study has implications for the selection of patients by psychiatrists and the type of treatment given to older adults.

3-28. Damrosch, S. P. (1984). Graduate nursing students' attitudes toward sexually active older persons. The Gerontologist, 24, 299-302.

A review of the literature on sexuality in older adults provides the introduction to this empirical study of 114 graduate nursing students. Each respondent read a vignette about a 68-year-old female. There were 6 versions of the story (wife, long-term widow, recent widow) in which the person was sexually active or inactive. The participants responded to a 10-item questionnaire. Results showed that the sexually active female was considered to be positive (cheerful, physically healthier, mentally alert, etc.). This study runs counter to other research that portrays sexually active older females negatively.

3-29. Dobrosky, B. J., & Bishop, J. M. (1986). Children's perceptions of old people. Educational Gerontology, 12, 429-439.

In this experiment 317 fourth and fifth graders enrolled in two suburban schools with differing socioeconomic traits (low and high income families), the participants were asked to describe what the term "an old person" meant to them. Results of this study paralleled earlier research. Students were limited to physical traits, associations with older relatives, problems, behavior, and age itself. Lower income participants were more positive in their assessment of older people. This research project indicates the range of categories that young children have for "old person." Evidence was not available about the criteria employed for this categorization.

3-30. Doka, K. J. (1985-1986). Adolescent attitudes and beliefs toward aging and the elderly. International Journal of Aging and Human Development, 22, 173-187.

In this study, 24 adolescents engaged in an oral history project in which they interviewed older adults. Prior to participating in the project the adolescents manifested a great deal of misinformation about older people. Despite enthusiastic involvement in the project, the participants failed to show any significant change in attitude toward older adults, and the aging process. Doka argues for more extensive intergenerational contacts in school curricula to help combat the misinformation about older people.

3-31. Fengler, A. P., & Wood, V. (1972). The generation gap: An analysis of attitudes on contemporary issues. The Gerontologist, 12 (2, part 1), 124-128.

In a study on value differences in 73 3-generation families (college student, parents, grandparents), the respondents (Catholics, Jews, Protestants) from the 3 generations were given a 50-item questionnaire on 8 separate scales: (1) distribution of economic and political influence; (2) reduction of the military; (3) patriotism versus protest; (4) the value of marriage; (5) sexuality and its boundaries; (6) religion; (7) use of marijuana; (8) toleration of minorities. Results indicated 2 general findings: (1) most issues involved 3 generations not just 2; and (2) age is the most consistent indicator of attitude differences. A replication of this study might prove interesting.

3-32. Fillmer, H. T. (1981). Sex stereotyping of the elderly by children. Educational Gerontology, 8, 77-85.

In this empirical analysis of children's attitudes, 2 classes each of grades 1-5 were sampled randomly to ascertain if children had a stereotypical attitude toward older adults. 166 boys and 175 girls participated in the experiment. The principal investigator interviewed each child who was shown a picture of a young man and a young woman as well as an old man and an old woman. Students were then asked a series of 6 questions to determine attitudes toward the people depicted in the pictures. The results showed that the children did, in fact, stereotype older people. Older men received a more negative response to the questions than did the older women. Likewise, girls were more willing to associate with older people than were boys. This study has important ramifications for the educational training of children.

3-33. Fillmer, H. T. (1984). Children's descriptions of and attitudes toward the elderly. Educational Gerontology, 10, 99-107.

144 children from grades 4 to 6 of a university laboratory school viewed four pictures (young man, young woman, older man, older woman). The subjects were then asked to evaluate (on a 5-point scale) the person in the picture on the basis of a number traits (sick-healthy, ugly-attractive, etc.). A set of questions was also posed (Would you greet the person in this picture?, etc.) Results of this experiment demonstrated several important points: (1) younger persons were more favorably evaluated; (2) men were rated more highly than women; (3) more positive responses resulted from question than to descriptive adjectival traits; and (4) younger people ranked higher in response to questions while older people were rated better on the adjectival trait scale. Fillmer offers 5 curricular suggestions to help eradicate stereotypical notions held by children.

3-34. Ford, C. V., & Sbordone, R. J. (1980). Attitudes of psychiatrists toward elderly patients. The American Journal of Psychiatry, 137, 571-575.

In response to a questionnaire sent to 350 practicing psychiatrists, 179 provided opinions about 4 clinical vignettes (2 dealt with an older patient, 2 with a young adult and a middle-aged person). The correlation of a patient's age and "idealness" was statistically significant. Likewise, the types of treatments prescribed differed according to the age of the patient.

3-35. Galbraith, M. W., & Suttie, S. M. (1987). Attitudes of nursing students toward the elderly. Educational Gerontology, 13, 213-223.

An evaluation of the attitude of 86 nursing students in an RN program toward older adults was measured by administering the Oberleder Attitude Toward Aging Scale both before and after a course with a gerontological component and a clinical nursing experience. Test results indicated a more positive shift in attitude. This study has implications for the nursing curriculum since courses with gerontology content and exposure to older patients seem to yield positive outcomes.

3-36. Green, S. (1981). Attitudes and perceptions about the elderly: Current and future perspectives. International Journal of Aging and Human Development, 13, 95-115.

Previous studies on attitudes and perceptions about older adults suffer from several problems: (1) lack of generalizability; (2) difficulties related to demand characteristics and social expectations; (3) psychometric quality. Issues related to stimuli and contexts, and the characteristics of perceivers are subsequently discussed in detail. Green offers specific recommendations to improve future research in items of stimulus and context variables and improved measurement.

3-37. Gresham, M. (1976). The infantilization of the elderly: A developing concept. Nursing Forum, 15, 196-211.

For the purposes of this study, the term infantilization means the treatment of older adults as children. The author argues that prevailing stereotypes create an environment for treating older people as children. Among the clinical examples noted are: (1) the application of child psychology to mature adults; (2) the use of the older person's first name by people in a position of authority; (3) imposition of punishment for non-compliance with regulations. Because the effects of this sort of subtle elder abuse is devastating, it must be identified and avoided. Further research is called for.

3-38. Gunter, L. M. (1971). Student's attitudes toward geriatric nursing. Nursing Outlook, 19, 466-469.

The Tuckman-Lorge Questionnaire was administered to 162 nursing students enrolled in a course entitled "Nursing Function in Gerontology" at the University of Washington School of Nursing. Results indicated that the nursing students had several stereotypes about older adults. This study points out an important problem in the preparation of nursing personnel, namely, the unwillingness of nursing students to work with a segment of the population that may need the most health care. The author advises the introduction of a course on gerontology into the curriculum during the last year of training.

3-39. Hauwiller, J. G., & Jennings, R. (1981). Counteracting age stereotyping with young school children. Educational Gerontology, 7, 183-190.

Workshops on gerontology for elementary school teachers (grades 2-4) were carried out across the state of Montana. 51 teachers participated in this program. A training manual with 50 topics for compositions on aging as well as other materials and suggestions formed part of this experience. The results show that teachers were enthusiastic about this topic, and follow up reports from the participants confirmed the success of this experimental program.

3-40. Hickey, T., Hickey, L. A., & Kalish, R. A. (1968). Children's perception of the elderly. The Journal of Genetic Psychology, 112, 227-235.

208 third-grade children from 4 different public and Catholic schools (2 from the upper socio-economic group, and 2 from the lower socio-economic stratum) in the greater Los Angeles area participated in this study. The students were

asked to write several sentences to describe an older person. 2 basic categories emerged from the experimental data: physical and social characteristics. Ambulatory differences were the most commonly reported physical difference. Positive social traits (friendliness) were reported 3 times more frequently than negative characteristics (meanness). A lower economic status of the subjects played a role in their negative evaluation of older people.

3-41. Hickey, T., & Kalish, R. (1968). Young people's perceptions of adults. Journal of Gerontology, 23, 215-219.

A total of 335 students from 4 age groups (78 third graders, 83 junior high school students, 102 high school students, 72 college undergraduates) with a gender balance were given a 20-item questionnaire about different age groups. Participants rated 4 adult age groups (25-, 45-, 65-, and 85-year-old people). Results indicated that children and young adults perceived differences between adult age groups. Moreover, such differences increase with age in terms of descriptive items but not for evaluative items. Finally, the older the individual, the less positive was the image of that person.

3-42. Holtzman, J. M., & Beck, J. D. (1979). Palmore's Facts on Aging Quiz: A reappraisal. The Gerontologist, 19, 116-120.

In a follow-up to Palmore's original discussion on his Facts on Aging Quiz (see 3-70) and Klemmack's response (see 3-51), Holtzman and Beck found that this instrument is useful for 3 of the purposes originally specified by Palmore: (1) encouragement of group discussions; (2) measurement and comparison of amounts of information held by distinct audiences; and (3) specification of most common misinformation about older people. Administration of this test to approximately 500 individuals failed to confirm that the quiz was an indirect measurement of prejudice toward older adults.

3-43. Isaacs, L. W., & Bearison, D. J. (1986). The development of children's prejudice against the aged. International Journal of Aging and Human Development, 23, 175-194.

In this experiment, 144 middle-class children (65 males, 79 females, ages 4, 6, 8) were administered The Social Attitude Scale of Ageist Prejudice. A total of 3 pilot studies involving 30 students each (10 from each age group). The children were told that they would work a puzzle with a job candidate who would work with children. Behavioral measures (proxemic distance, productivity in completing the puzzle, eye-contact, verbal interaction, initiation of conversation, number of words) of social attitudes were employed to determine the children's reactions. Only the 4-year-olds failed to demonstrate stereotypic views of older people. Likewise, older women were perceived more negatively than older men. This study indicates that by the time children reach school age, they have already adopted negative attitudes toward older people. Further research on this phenomenon is necessary.

3-44. Jantz, R. K., Seefeldt, C., Galper, A., & Serock, K. (1977). Children's attitudes toward the elderly. Social Education, 41, 518-522.

This study sought answers to questions about children's knowledge about feelings toward, contacts with, and perceptions of their own aging and the process of aging itself. The C[hildren's] A[ttitudes] T[oward the] E[lderly] assessment instrument designed in 1976 by the authors of this article was the testing instrument used in this experiment. The CATE includes four sub-tests: (1) word association modification; (2) semantic differential test; (3) a series of pictures; and (4) A Piaget format designed to evaluate a child's cognitive development status. 180 children aged 3-11 (20 from each age group) participated in this evaluation. Results were mixed. Children demonstrated generally positive affective feelings toward older people. Nevertheless, the subjects had negative emotions about the physical aspect of older people and about growing older themselves. The authors specify a set of goals for creating positive attitudes toward older people and their own aging.

3-45. Kastenbaum, C. (1972). The reluctant therapist. Geriatrics, 18, 296-301.

The thesis of this essay is that psychotherapists avoid older clients. Among the factors that contribute to the reluctancy of therapists to treat older people include the desire to treat people with a high social status. Next, the clinician's personality plays a role in the treatment of older people. The treatment of older adults often forces the psychotherapist to face his or her own death--a grim prospect for many. Another factor is a conflict in values. A recognition that older adults may not live long raises questions in the mind of the therapist about the limited value of such treatment. Finally, an illogical focus on the future and long-term therapeutic benefits argues against treatment of the older client.

3-46. Katz, R. S. (1990). Personality trait correlates of attitudes toward older people. International Journal of Aging and Human Development, 31, 147-159.

In this study, an examination of the relationship between personality and attitudes toward older adults was carried out. The participants were 228 students and gerontology practitioners who completed the Aging Opinion Survey, the Cattell 16 Personalities Test, and a demographic questionnaire. The results showed that a constellation of characteristics corresponded to attitudes toward older adults, namely, low anxiety traits, sensitive-intuition traits, and intellectual ability. This experiment implies that to change negative attitudes toward older people, it is necessary to reduce anxieties about growing old. Thus, understanding the sources of negative attitudes is one way of combating this form of prejudice.

3-47. Kayser, J. S., & Minnigerode, F. A. (1975). Increasing nursing students' interest in working with aged patients. Nursing Research, 24, 23-26.

Administration of the Tuckman-Lorge Questionnaire to 311 baccalaureate nursing students enrolled at the University of San Francisco yielded results that were substantially similar to those of Gunter (see 3-38). Particularly alarming was the fact that even those students who had had previous contact with geriatric patients were unwilling to continue in that domain. Demographic trends suggest that the nursing profession will have an increased need for personnel to care for older adults. To combat the negative attitudes of nursing students, these researchers propose to alter current curricula by including clinical experiences in geriatric settings such as nursing homes.

3-48. Kearl, M. C. (1981-1982). An inquiry into the positive personal and social effects of old age stereotypes among the elderly. International Journal of Aging and Human Development, 14, 277-290.

Using the notion of relative advantage in contradistinction to relative deprivation, Kearl sought to determine if negative stereotypes, in fact, enhance participation and support for organizations for older adults through a syndrome of denial opposition. The results of this study indicate that older adults are willing to participate in organizations, and are willing to increase taxes for all age groups to support older people.

3-49. Kent, D. P. (1965). Aging--fact and fancy. The Gerontologist, 2, 51-56, 111.

Emphasis on long-term solutions to the issues of older adults and aging is called for in this essay. Far too often, however, superficial resolutions are provided. Kent calls upon his colleagues to rid themselves of stereotypical views of old age and older people, and to begin to deal with the real problems.

3-50. Kilty, K. M., & Feld, A. (1976). Attitudes toward aging and toward the needs of older people. Journal of Gerontology, 31, 586-594.

A factor analysis of 2 sets of opinion statements (attitudes toward aging, programmatic issues) were administered to 2 distinct age groups: People under

60 (N=290); and people over 60 (N=181).   Results indicated that older people's responses were more complex and varied than those of younger people.

3-51. Klemmack, D. L. (1978). Comment: An examination of Palmore's Facts on Aging Quiz. The Gerontologist, 18, 403-406.

Klemmack employed Palmore's Facts on Aging Quiz on a random sample of 202 adults residing in a southern city. This essay attacks Palmore's quiz because it found that 7 items with highest and lowest scores failed to meet the usual standards for tests. The author states that the Facts on Aging Quiz is inadequate as a research tool to ascertain level of knowledge of aging (see 3-70).

3-52. Kogan, N. (1961). Attitudes toward old people: The development of a scale and an examination of correlates. Journal of Abnormal and Social Psychology, 62(1), 44-54.

This study is a proposal for a Likert scale evaluation instrument to ascertain attitudes toward older adults. The author concluded that no correlation existed between an authoritarian personality and attitudes toward older people. Likewise, people with negative views of minority groups and physically challenged people had a much more unfavorable disposition toward older people. Finally, subjects who scored as highly nurturant on a psychological test had a more positive conception of older people.

3-53. Kogan, N. (1979a). Beliefs, attitudes and stereotypes about old people: A new look at some old issues. Research on Aging, 1, 12-36.

This essay addresses conceptual and methodological questions about beliefs, attitudes, and stereotypes of older adults ignored previously. Kogan argues that most of the extant research on this subject is theoretical. Instruments and techniques of evaluation have been favored over processes and constructs. The author believes that this situation will, however, soon change.

3-54. Kogan, N. (1979b). A study of age categorization. Journal of Gerontology, 34, 358-367.

In this empirical study, Kogan asked 150 subjects (5 groups each of 15 males and females) in different age groups (18-21, 22-28, 29-38, 39-55, 56-76) to estimate chronological age for 2 sets of 33 photos (male and female). Respondents rated the photos in adolescent, young, middle-aged, elderly and aged adult, as well as for preference. Results indicated that the person's sex influenced evaluation, e.g., more females were judged to be older. Likewise, in the preference data, preferred male or female persons were judged to be younger than depicted. No bias was detected in the oldest and the youngest respondents.

3-55. Kosberg, J. L., & Gorman, J. F. (1975). Perceptions toward the care of institutionalized aged. The Gerontologist, 15, 398-403.

A 29-item questionnaire developed for this study was designed to assess perceptions of rehabilitation potential of older adults by those associated with a home for older adults. Different perceptions corresponded to role category of the individual (social worker, professional nurse, secretary, therapist, non-professional nurse, housekeeper, volunteer), and years of education.

3-56. Kremer, J. F. (1988). Effects of negative information about aging on attitudes. Educational Gerontology, 14, 69-80.

In this study, 30 undergraduate students enrolled in a psychology course were selected (N=30, 18 females, 12 males). The subjects were administered 2 attitude scales (Attitudes Toward Older Adults, life-satisfaction questions from the Tuckman-Lorge test). The participants were subdivided into 3 different groups. The results of this study indicated that students who had slightly negative attitudes toward older adults showed no change when presented with negative information about older people, though they did exhibit a more negative attitude about themselves. However, when presented with factual information about aging, the attitudes of the participants toward older adults and themselves improved.

3-57. Leiffer, J. (1982). Eight reasons why doctors fear the elderly, chronic illness, and death. The Journal of Transpersonal Psychology, 14, 47-60.

In this essay, Leiffer seeks to explain why physicians have a fear of older adults, chronic illness, mortality which he labels a self-defeating attitude since some people will face at least one of these situations at some point. The reasons for this fear include: (1) ageism; (2) the morbid nature of discussing death; (3) the complex nature of patient problems; (4) physicians' unresolved fears about their own aging; (5) ignorance about the final stages of life; (6) the lack of a spiritual element in psychotherapy; (7) the omnipotent role often assigned a medical doctor; and (8) the sense of impotence related to incurable maladies. These attitudes are the result of medical training deficiencies but this situation can be changed.

3-58. Levin, W. C. (1988). Age stereotyping: College student evaluations. Research on Aging, 10, 134-148.

An experiment with college students from California, Massachusetts, and Tennessee in which the participants (170 subjects from each sample) evaluated a photograph (the picture represented a 25-, 52-, and 73-year-old individual) based on a short vignette about this person. The students then responded to a 19-item questionnaire. Results indicated that older people continue to be evaluated stereotypically on the basis of characteristics presumed to be associated with age.

3-59. Linden, M. E. (1957, February). Effects of social attitudes on the mental health of the aging. Geriatrics, 109-114.

In this essay, Linden discusses certain problems associated with the mental health of older adults. The major points discussed are: (1) loneliness; (2) a loss of identity; (3) the emphasis placed on physical beauty in this culture.

3-60. Lubomudrov, S. (1987). Congressional perceptions of the elderly: The use of stereotypes in the legislative process. The Gerontologist, 27, 77-81.

A content analysis of congressional documents on the Reagan Social Security recommendations (May 12-December 19, 1981) was employed to determine legislator's perceptions of older adults. Two sources were accessed (hearings by the Senate Special Committee on Aging, the House Select Committee on Aging, the Subcommittee on Social Security and Income Maintenance Programs of the Senate Finance Committee, and the House Subcommittee on Ways and Means) and the Congressional Record. This investigation revealed that negative and positive stereotypes exist among congressional representatives. Lubomudrov concludes that the greatest political support for older adults is to be found among politicians with misperceptions of this group.

3-61. McTavish, D. G. (1971). Perceptions of old people: A review of research findings. The Gerontologist, 11, 90-101.

In this comprehensive review of the literature on the perception of older adults, McTavish notes that studies of this type differ in 2 crucial ways. One trend is the culture or society as the unit of analysis, while the other focuses on individual or analytic sub-groups. The author suggests future areas for research such as cross-age comparisons, longitudinal studies of different social settings, the creation of methods that utilize linguistic analysis and the development of non-verbal evaluation instruments. McTavish warns that perceptions of older people are not static or unidimensional, therefore, measurements must account for this aspect.

3-62. Matthews, S. (1979). The social world of old women: Management of self-identity. Beverly Hills, CA: Sage Publications.

This study deals with how older women are treated in this society. Several of the chapters deal with the problems older women face because of the stereotypes about older women perpetuated in this society. Although the statistical information about the situation of older women is dated, many of the premises remain true.

3-63. Menks, F. (1983). The use of a board game to simulate the experiences of old age. The Gerontologist, 23, 565-568.

The Road to Life, a board game designed to increase understanding and comprehension of certain psychological and physical experiences of old age was developed by the author for use in an Applied Human Growth and Development class. The game takes 25 minutes to play, and is followed by group discussion. This game and has been field-tested with people aged 10 to 93, and stimulates dialogue about a number of gerontological issues.

3-64. Miller, R. B., & Dodder, R. A. (1980). A revision of Palmore's Facts on Aging Quiz. The Gerontologist, 20, 673-679.

In this revision of Palmore's Facts on Aging Quiz, the authors suggest revision for items, 3, 5, 11, 13, 17, 21, 24. The original Palmore items and the revision were placed side by side in a chart for comparison. The revised format was then used on 430 college students. The authors argue that their edited version of the Palmore quiz both supports and improves it (see 3-70).

3-65. Mitchell, J., Wilson, K., Revicki, D., & Parker, L. (1985). Children's perceptions of aging: A multidimensional approach to differences by age, sex, and race. The Gerontologist, 25, 182-187.

A 25-item index designed to measure children's perceptions toward older adults was administered to 255 black (125) and white (130), male (124) and female (131) children from North Carolina aged to 5 to 13. Photographic sketches of 3 age groups (young adult, middle-aged, older adult), male and female, black and white were presented to the participants to determine different areas: (1) personality traits; (2) affective relations; and (3) physical capabilities. The results indicated that there was little racial or gender difference in attitudes. Moreover, the children view older people positively, albeit with diminished physical ability. Likewise, what the child considers to be important plays a role in the assessment of older people.

3-66. Mitchell, J., & Mathews, H. F. (1987). Perceptions of older adults: Differences by age and sex among children in a Costa Rican community. International Journal of Aging and Human Development, 25, 223-238.

In this study, the authors interviewed 120 Afro-Caribbean children from a rural Costa Rican town. The children were shown sketches of males and females that represented younger, middle-aged, and older adults. In this community, middle-aged and older women were seen to be more authoritative, while older men were viewed as more affective. This study contrasts with industrialized societies where older people are excluded from power and control of goods with the result that they are unlikely to be considered authoritative or powerful. In addition to survey results, the authors employed ethnographic techniques.

3-67. Murphy-Russell, S., Die., A. H., & Walker, J. L., Jr. (1986). Changing attitudes toward the elderly: The impact of three methods of attitude change. Educational Gerontology, 12, 241-251.

In this experiment, 3 instructional techniques were employed to determine the effectiveness of procedures designed to change attitudes toward older adults. These techniques included: (1) peer discussion; (2) personal contact with the attitude object; and (3) augmentation of knowledge about the subject. Results indicate that the most successful strategy was direct contact with older people. Nevertheless, the other 2 groups also registered more positive attitudes toward older people after their participation in this program. The Attitudes Toward Old People Scale was the pre- and post-test measurement instrument. A total of 84 college students (ages 17-25) participated in this experiment.

3-68. Neugarten, B. L., & Garron, D. C. (1959, January). Attitudes of middle-aged persons toward growing older. Geriatrics, 21-24.

A Kansas City survey of 625 men and women (ages 40-70) about their attitudes toward aging. Results indicate the following about current views: (1) neutral attitude (55%); (2) positive attitude (28%); and (3) negative attitude (17%). Future views were fairly similar (neutral--55%, positive--14%, negative--13%, contingent--18%). The implications of this study suggest that gerontologists need to consider social and psychological processes relevant to aging rather than a simple chronological approach.

3-69. Page, S., Olivas, R., Driver, J., & Driver, R. (1981). Children's attitudes toward the elderly and aging. Educational Gerontology, 7, 43-47.

144 students (71 girls, 73 boys) from nursery school to grade 6 (ages 3 to 11) were evaluated to determine their attitudes toward older adults. The researchers

reported generally negative results based on prevalent stereotypes about older people. This situation derives from limited intergenerational contact. Stereotypical views of older adults appear to develop quite early. Therefore, changes in such attitudes must be effected in very early childhood.

3-70. Palmore, E. B. (1977). The Facts on Aging: A short quiz. The Gerontologist, 17, 315-320.

Designed as an alternative to existing assessment instruments on aging, Palmore's quiz is short, contains only factual statements as opposed to attitudinal statements, and the factual material is documented. The author provides a sample of his Facts on Aging Quiz in this article. It has 25 true-false statements. Factually-documented answers are then provided. Uses of this quiz promoting discussion, assessment of ageist prejudice, isolation of prevalent misconceptions about older adults, measurement of effects of classes devoted to aging, and shifts in public opinion.

3-71. Palmore, E. B. (1978a). Are the aged a minority group? Journal of American Geriatric Society, 26, 214-217.

The question raised by Streib (see 3-94) about the minority status of older adults is addressed in this article. Streib proposed 5 questions to determine if a group constituted a minority. Palmore discusses systematically these 5 criteria, concluding that a simple yes or no response is impossible. The author speculates about the future of older people and hypothesizes that a trend toward an age-irrelevant society.

3-72. Palmore, E. B. (1978b). Professor Palmore responds. The Gerontologist, 18, 405-406.

This refutation of an article (see 3-51) on the author's Facts on Aging Quiz, Palmore points out that his instrument is not psychometric but "edumetric."

3-73. Palmore, E. B. (1980). The Facts on Aging Quiz: A review of findings. The Gerontologist, 20, 659-672.

This report summarizes more than 25 studies which have appeared since the publication of Palmore's groundbreaking Facts on Aging Quiz (see 3-70). Findings include: (1) group reliability is high yet item reliability is low; (2) amount of education affects scores; (3) gerontology training helps test scores; and (4) erroneous beliefs are identified.

3-74. Palmore, E. B. (1981). The Facts on Aging Quiz: Part two. The Gerontologist, 21, 431-437.

A different Facts on Aging Quiz is presented in this article. Although the questions in this test are different, its purpose is similar to the first (see 3-70), i.e., to measure attitudes and changes in test-takers, to facilitate discussion, and to clarify erroneous beliefs about older adults.

3-75. Palmore, E. B. (1981). More on Palmore's Facts on Aging Quiz. The Gerontologist, 21, 115-116.

This is an answer to a suggestion for revision of the author's Facts on Aging Quiz (see 3-64). Palmore agrees that 5 of the proposals will improve his instrument slightly. Nevertheless, 2 additional changes are shown to be wrong.

3-76. Palmore, E. B. (1982). Attitudes toward the aged. Research on Aging, 4, 333-348.

A review of the literature on attitudes toward the aged is extensive. Available studies employ a variety of different approaches (societal studies, agree-disagree scales, semantic differential scales, contents analysis methods, NCOA Survey, the Facts on Aging Quiz). In a discussion of needed research, Palmore specifies a sound theoretical model with large national samples, high reliability and validity, use of multiple-choice, age-period-cohort analysis, and cost-benefit analysis.

3-77. Palmore, E. B. (1988). The Facts on Aging Quiz: A handbook of uses and results. New York: Springer Publishing Company.

This volume contains 7 chapters which include the following: (1) updated versions of Palmore's original Facts on Aging Quizzes from The Gerontologist (see 3-70, 3-74); (2) an entirely new Facts on Aging quiz about mental health; (3) a guide on how to use the quizzes; (4) the results of studies in which these testing instruments have been used; (5) an assessment of the uses of Palmore's quizzes by C. M. Barresi and T. H. Brubaker; (6) a summary and exploration of future directions. The second part of this book contains a useful set of abstracts on studies that have used the quizzes. References and an Index complement this work. The now famous Facts on Aging Quizzes educate the people who take it to better understand older adults through factual accounts of who they are. This test functions to eliminate stereotypic attitudes.

3-78. Parnell, K. (1980). Younger and old together: A literature review. Childhood Education, 56, 184-188.

This essay provides an overview of three aspects of intergenerational contacts: (1) attitudes of younger people toward older adults; (2) programs to transform children's attitudes and beliefs about older people and aging; and (3) the curricular implication of educational materials on this subject.

3-79. Ray, D. C., McKinney, K. A., & Ford, C. V. (1987). Differences in psychologists' ratings of older and younger clients. The Gerontologist, 27, 82-86.

407 licensed clinical psychologists from Tennessee received a test instrument (192 responses, 47.4%) that included 4 vignettes (clients described showed symptoms of mania, depression, agoraphobia, and alcohol abuse). The respondents were asked to comment on several points: (1) the idealness of the client; (2) prognosis; and (3) recommended treatment. Results indicated that older patients who were depressed or manic received poorer prognoses than younger clients. Older psychologists, however, rated older clients more positively in terms of idealness. This study indicates that psychologists must become aware of understanding their own attitudes toward the older client in order to provide better clinical treatment.

3-80. Rodin, J., & Langer, E. (1980). Aging labels: The decline of control and the fall of self-esteem. Journal of Social Issues, 26(2), 12-29.

In this review essay, the authors examine previous research that has examined the relationship of negative labeling to a decrease in control and reduction in self-esteem. The first group of studies examines the effects of negative labels. Other research deals with the effects of age-relevant labels on the behavior of older adults. In their conclusion, the authors argue that conscious-raising about older adults must create opportunities for increased self-esteem and self-control. Moreover, social change must foster real control and not the perception of control.

3-81. Rosencranz, H. A. & McNevin, T. E. (1969). A factor analysis of attitudes toward the aged. The Gerontologist, 9, 55-59.

A semantic differential analytical instrument was devised which consisted of bipolar adjectives to describe behavioral traits of people of all ages. This test was subsequently administered to 200 young adults (aged 17-21). In each case, the subjects were asked to evaluate a male from 3 different age groups (20-30, 40-55, 70-85). Results showed that the older male was judged to be instrumentally ineffective, more dependent, though personally acceptable. Those respondents with qualitative and quantitative contact with older adults showed a more positive attitude toward the older male.

3-82. Ross, R. F., Jr., & Freitag, C. B. (1976). A comparison of adolescent and adult attitudes toward the aged. Educational Gerontology, 1, 291-295.

A test that employed a semantic differential analysis was administered to 70 adolescents, and 65 young adults. The test included items along stereotypic lines (autonomous-dependent, instrumental-ineffective, personal acceptability-unacceptability) with 32 bipolar adjectival sets. Results of the experiment showed that the adolescents demonstrated more positive attitudes toward older adults than did the young adults. The authors argue that more education will improve attitudes toward older adults. Moreover, attitudinal transformations would improve the situation of older adults and prevent the sense of dread that young people harbor about growing old.

3-83. Ryan, E. B., & Capadano, H. L., III. (1978). Age perceptions and evaluative reaction toward adult speakers. Journal of Gerontology, 33, 98-102.

2 experiments were designed to determine the attitudes of listeners toward a speaker perceived to be old. 98 Notre Dame undergraduates participated in this study. The subjects listened to 16 different recordings of a brief passage by females (12-71 years of age), and 16 males (17-68 years of age). Results indicate that older females are judged as reserved, passive, inflexible, and "out-of-it," while older males are perceived as less flexible than their younger counterparts. This form of indirect evaluation of age stereotypes is promising.

3-84. Ryan, E. B., & Johnston, D. G. (1987). The influence of communication effectiveness on evaluation of older and younger speakers. Journal of Gerontology, 42, 163-164.

80 undergraduate students (57 women, 23 men) listened to 2 taped conversations of instructions for directions recorded by younger and older males. Results indicated that communication effectiveness was the significant factor in assessing competence, and not the age of the speaker.

3-85. Schonfield, D. (1982). Who is stereotyping whom and why? The Gerontologist, 22, 267-272.

Skepticism about the trend by gerontologists to imply that negative attitudes toward older adults prevail in America. Schonfield attributes this widely held belief to terminological confusion, i.e., key terms (ageism, prejudice, attitude, belief, etc.) are ambiguous or have distinct connotations for different people. The author concludes his essay by questioning the motives of some researchers engaged in gerontological investigations.

3-86. Seccombe, K., & Ishii-Kuntz, M. (1991). Perceptions of problems associated with aging: Comparisons among four older age cohorts. The Gerontologist, 31, 527-533.

In this experiment 4 age cohorts: (1) middle-aged (55-64); (2) young old (65-74); (3) old (75-84); and (4) oldest old (85+), attitudes toward the special problems faced by older adults was measured. The data base consisted of 2,329 persons over the age of 55 who responded to a questionnaire. The results showed that the middle-aged group was most pessimistic, while the oldest old were unexpectedly optimistic despite the fact that members of this group may face more difficulties associated with old age. The authors speculate that personal attitudes determine one's perceptions. This study supports the contention that younger people hold a more pessimistic attitude toward than do older people themselves.

3-87. Seefeldt, C. (1984). Children's attitudes toward the elderly: A cross-cultural comparison. International Journal of Aging and Human Development, 19, 319-328.

In an experiment designed to test the hypothesis that U.S. children's negative attitudes toward older adults are unique, the author administered the Children's Attitudes Toward the Elderly test to 4 groups of 4th, 5th, 6th grade children in the Aleutian Islands (N=29), Asuncion, Paraguay (N=69), Australia (N=39), and mainland U.S. (N=60). The Semantic Differential subtest of the CATE was used to assess attitudes of the participants. Results of this experiment indicate that all 4 groups tested held negative views about older adults. The author concludes by cautioning that these are preliminary results based on a small sample.

3-88. Seefeldt, C., Jantz, R. K., Galper, A., & Serock, K. (1977). Children's attitudes toward the elderly: Educational implications. Educational Gerontology, 2, 301-310.

The Children's Attitude Toward the Elderly test was administered to 180 school children (20 each for ages 3 to 11). Few children evaluated their own old age positively. Likewise, these subjects did not hold old age in general as positive. These findings imply that accurate information about older adults as well as intergenerational contact are necessary to combat these attitudes.

3-89. Seefeldt, C. Jantz, R. K., Galper, A., & Serock, K. (1977). Using pictures to explore children's attitudes toward the elderly. The Gerontologist, 17, 506-512.

An empirical test of 180 children (20 at each of 9 grade levels from nursery school to grade 6) was carried out to assess attitudes toward older adults. The testing instrument consisted of 4 black-and-white photos of a man previously judged to be 30.1, 44.5, 63.7, and 77.4 years of age respectively. Respondents were asked to assess the person's age, and to make additional comments about activities that might be done with the person depicted. Results indicated that children comprehend the notion of "old." Evaluation of the oldest man produced the most negative comments related to physical, and behavioral traits. The authors note that these results have curricular implications for exposure of children to realistic experiences with older people to combat stereotypes in future generations.

3-90. Shanas, E. (1979). Social myth as hypothesis: The case of the family relations of old people. The Gerontologist, 19, 3-9.

The author seeks to debunk the commonly held belief that old people as a group suffer from alienation from their families and their children. Such erroneous notions tend to shape society's attitudes toward older adults unless they are disproven. Shanas succeeds in refuting systematically all of the myths of alienation (mobil society, alienation of older and younger people, predominance of the nuclear family, and an extensive human services systems). The author argues for more research on this subject including childless old adults, the role of kinfolk, as well as other issues.

3-91. Sheppard, H. L. (1990). Damaging stereotypes about aging are taking hold: How to counter them? Perspective on Aging, 19, 4-8.

The stereotypic depiction of older adults as "elderly, affluent--and selfish" is denounced in this essay. The source of this incorrect characterization of older people derives from a false belief that entitlement programs such as Social Security are draining resources from the young. The effect is to foment intergenerational conflict. This article effectively challenges many misconceptions about this inflammatory issue.

3-92. Solomon, K., & Vickers, R. (1979). Attitudes of health workers toward old people. Journal of the American Geriatrics Society, 27, 186-191.

The Tuckman-Lorge Questionnaire on attitudes toward older adults and aging was administered to 3 groups of health care workers: (1) medical students;

(2) housestaff members; and (3) members of a mobile psychogeriatric team. The geriatric personnel demonstrated the fewest stereotypes with the result that their patients received good care. Nevertheless, overall results indicate that few changes have taken place since the first test results were published by Tuckman and Lorge in 1953.

3-93. Spence, P. L. (1968). Medical student attitudes toward the geriatric patient. Journal of the American Geriatrics Society, 16, 976-983.

First and fourth year students enrolled at the University of California Medical School were given questionnaires designed to determine their attitudes toward older patients. Response rates were significantly different for freshmen (92 of 117) and seniors (46 of 102). Results of this survey indicate that both groups hold stereotypes of geriatric clients. This means that for the senior medical student, 3 years of medical education had done nothing to change such prejudiced values.

3-94. Streib, G. F. (1968). Are the aged a minority group? In B. Neugarten (Ed.), Middle age and aging: A reader in social psychology (pp. 35-46). Chicago: University of Chicago Press.

The issue of whether older people constitute a minority group is controversial. In this essay, Streib reviews 6 criteria that determine minority status (entire life cycle, majority group stereotypes, group identity, willingness to organize as a political group, differing access to power and status, deprivation). Older adults possess all but the first identifying characteristic for legitimate recognition as a minority group. Since old age is not a recognizable trait for the entire life cycle, this group, according to the author, fails to meet the necessary requisites for minority status.

3-95. Thomas, W. C., Jr. (1981). The expectation gap and the stereotype of the stereotype: Images of old people. The Gerontologist, 21, 402-407.

In this response to Shanas' essay (see 3-90) on alienation as a social myth, Thomas seeks to clarify the stereotype issue. The author discusses the notion of "expectation gap" by which he means the difference between what older people have and what the members of this group believe they should have. If older adults have appropriate expectations, they will contribute to their own well-being.

3-96. Tibbitts, C. (1979). Can we invalidate negative stereotypes of aging? The Gerontologist, 19, 10-19.

In this Donald W. Kent Memorial Lecture presented at the annual meeting of the Gerontological Society of America, the challenge of combating erroneous stereotypes of older adults is addressed. General subjects reviewed are the origin of stereotypes, positive perceptions of older people, and their roles in work, volunteerism, family, and citizenship and advocacy. Tibbitts believes that some of the trends in society are helping the erosion of negative stereotypes about aging and older adults in this society. This essay is an excellent panorama of the situation of older people in 1978. An evaluative follow-up study would be valuable.

3-97. Tuckman, J., & Lorge, I. (1953a). Attitudes toward old people. Journal of Social Psychology, 37, 249-260.

This much cited study reports on an experiment intended to ascertain the attitudes of young graduate students toward older adults. A questionnaire that dealt with issues such as physical change, personality traits, conservatism, resistance to change, and interpersonal relationships contained a total of 137 statements. The testing instrument was administered to 147 graduate students (92 men, 55 women). Results confirmed that substantial stereotypical perceptions about older people existed among the subjects tested. The authors concluded that older people live in a society that holds this group in very low esteem.

3-98. Tuckman, J., & Lorge, I. (1953b). 'When aging begins' and stereotypes about aging. Journal of Gerontology, 8, 489-492.

The authors focus on 2 specific questions about aging from 2 different questionnaires--one with 137 items, the other with 51 items. The questions are: (1) "In your opinion when does old age begin;" and (2) "in your opinion when is a worker old?" Results indicate that those respondents who use chronological age as a criterion harbor more stereotypes about older people. The authors argue for the abandonment of age chronology as a criterion for the notion of "old." Instead, suitable objective criteria must be established.

3-99. Warren, D. L., & Painter, A., & Rudisill, J. (1983). Effects of geriatric education on the attitudes of medical students. Journal of the American Geriatric Society, 31, 435-438.

The participants in this study were 80 third-year medical students (79% males, 21% female, average age 28) from Wright State University (Dayton, Ohio). All students were administered the Geriatric Attitude Survey prior to participating in a 25 hour geriatric education segment of the family practice clerkship. Results showed that this program had a positive impact on the students as measured by a second administration of the Geriatric Attitude Survey. Of the 4 attitudinal categories measured (personal anxiety about aging, social value of older adults, geriatric patient care, stereotypical view about older people), the area of stereotypic attitudes toward this group revealed the most significant improvement. Finally, prior experience in geriatric medicine showed a positive correlation with positive attitudes toward older people.

3-100. Wolff, K. (1957, February). Definition of the geriatric patient. Geriatrics, 102-106.

This definition of the "geriatric patient" paints a very negative picture of such an individual. Such clients represent a "social problem." According to Wolff, a geriatric patient suffers from a "decline of intellectual faculties, and a lack of emotional equilibrium." This description leaves little doubt as to why medical school graduates would eschew a practice with this kind of clientele.

3-101. Wolk, R. L., & Wolk, R. B. (1971). Professional workers' attitudes toward the aged. Journal of the American Geriatric Society, 19, 624-639.

A total of 300 questionnaires was sent to professionals (social service workers, psychologists, nurses) with 231 returns (11 of which were discarded because they were incomplete). An item-by-item analysis of the questionnaire takes up most of this paper. Among the general results are the following: (1) the older professional idealizes the older patient and becomes disenchanted with the real person; (2) the older worker is threatened by the dependency of the older client; (3) the younger professional fails to identify readily with the older patient.

3-102. Youmans, E. G. (1977). Attitudes: Young-old and old-old. The Gerontologist, 17, 175-179.

Differentiation of age groups in industrial societies is increasing rapidly. In this study of 266 respondents (172 women, 94 men), subjective attitudes of well-being by young-old, and old-old were shown to correspond to the type of community (urban versus rural). The results showed that urban old-old were more satisfied with their situation than were rural old-old people.

3-103. Zandi, T., Mirle, J., & Jarvis, P. (1990). Children's attitudes toward elderly individuals: A comparison of two ethnic groups. International Journal of Aging and Human Development, 30, 161-174.

Attitudes of Indian children born in the U.S., and American children toward older adults were assessed in this study by using the Children's Attitudes Toward the Elderly test. Results of the test showed that Indian children tended to give behavioral responses more than the American children who engaged in affective and cognitive responses.   The authors suggest that research which compares Indian children born in this country and those born in India may provide important new information.

3-104. Zimring, J. G. (1977). Physician and geriatric patient. New York State Journal of Medicine, 6, 968-970.

The author cites some of the problems associated with the treatment of geriatric patients such as errors of over- and under-diagnosis, and a general disinterest in or distaste for this type of practice.   Suggested remedies for this situation include geriatrics as a specialty in medicine with increased training in diagnostic procedures, education in the natural changes in the aging body, and a more humanistic approach to medical education for the medical student.

4

COMMUNICATION

4-1. Aday, R. H. (1991). Important functions of the gerontological newsletter. Educational Gerontology, 17, 315-322.

A review of 13 different gerontological newsletters revealed the following information: (1) a typology of newsletters (aging center, organization, independent); (2) content analysis (essay briefs, research and training information, resource materials, exemplary programs). The gerontology newsletter serves various functions including a source of discussion, an educational resource, and an information item for bulletin boards. Aday suggests areas for future research into additional uses of this type of communication tool.

4-2. Aldridge, G. J. (1976). Lifelong education and the aging: Opportunities for communicating. In H. J. Oyer, & E. J. Oyer (Eds.) Aging and communication (pp. 187-203). Baltimore, MD: University Park Press.

Because education is now considered to be a lifelong process, Aldridge advocates the development of continuing education for older adults. Research indicates that age is no barrier to learning. Development of appropriate education programs for older people requires preparation, commitment, and personnel skilled in effective communication with this age group. Attention must be paid to the special instructional interests of older people.

4-3.   The American Jewish Committee.   (1978).   Image of old age in the American Media. New York: The American Jewish Committee.

This set of conference proceedings held at Columbia University on December 8, 1977 summarizes the general topics of the symposium: (1) Today's images; (2) Formats and Topics (television, television commercials, news coverage, PSAs, special programming); (3) why the media are that way; (4) change in the air; and (5) how to do it better. In addition, abstracts of 2 speakers (W. P. Davidson, N. H. Cruickshank) are reproduced.

4-4. Atkin, C. K. (1976). Mass media and the aging. In H. J. Oyer, & E. J. Oyer (Eds.) Aging and communication (pp. 99-118).   Baltimore, MD: University Park Press.

Older adults spend 3 to 6 hours per day with the various mass media (television, radio, newspapers). Their use of the mass media includes information, entertainment, and surrogate social interactions. Despite this information, little is known about the effect of the mass media on older people. Social scientific research questions relating to the mass media and older people that require further investigation include: (1) the mass media usage patterns of television by older adults; (2) the context of its consumption; (3) what is the effect of programming and stereotyping on older adults? In the realm of applied research, additional information is needed: (1) what are the programming needs of older people?; (2) how do older adults evaluate the media?; (3) what print media techniques serve the needs of older people?

4-5. Barton, R. L., & Schreiber, E. (1978). Media and aging: A critical review of an expanding field of communication research. Central States Speech Journal, 29, 173-186.

This overview of research on the relationship between aging and the mass media. There are several major areas of investigation: (1) media-use behavior and demography of the older adult audience; (2) content analyses of the media; (3) effects of the media on individual reactions to aging; (4) the social dimensions of the interrelationships of the media and the aging process; (5) the structural and functional aspects of the media's influence on aging; (6) approaches to using the media in issues relating to aging.

4-6. Bayles, K. A., & Kaszniak, A. W. (1987). Communication and cognition in normal aging and dementia. Boston: A College-Hill Publication, Little, Brown, and Company.

This textbook focuses on speech disfluencies in older adults. In this sense, its focus is on the deviation from a putative speech norm to be found in the older person. Specific chapters treat dementia and aphasia in older patients. The fifth chapter, however, discusses the topic of linguistic communication and normal aging. The book is a well-written, well-documented, and comprehensive reference work for the clinician. See 4-36.

4-7. Beattie, W. M., Jr. (1976). The relevance of communication for professionals involved with the elderly: Focus on social workers. In H. J. Oyer, & E. J. Oyer (Eds.) Aging and communication (pp. 239-251). Baltimore, MD: University Park Press.

Professional caregivers have only begun to realize that older adults form a sub-clientele that requires specialized services. Social workers in particular need to pay attention to the needs of this group. Communication with older people requires specialized knowledge of generational differences, individual differences, and age-related changes. In addition, appropriate strategies are necessary to communicate with the members of this group. Much more research will be necessary to develop effective procedures for communication between the older client and the social worker.

4-8. Benjamin, B. J. (1986). Dimensions of the older female voice. Language & Communication, 6, 45-55.

Research into changes in voice has focused on the male. In general, there are several features that distinguish the male and female voice, namely, pitch, inflection, and absolute vowel format frequencies. In this study, Benjamin selected 40 speakers who were divided into 4 subgroups (10 older females aged 69-82, 10 older males aged 68-81, 10 females aged 21-32, 10 males aged 23-32). Each one read "The Rainbow Passage" from G. Fairbanks Voice and articulation drillbook (1960) (New York: Harper Brothers), which was recorded and played for 12 speech pathology graduate students who evaluated characteristics of the aging voice (pitch, rate of speech, loudness, nasality, and other factors). This experiment considered not only the changes in voice quality but also the effects on the listener. Certain personality traits were attributed to older females on the basis of voice, e.g., less active personality, reduced femininity, and negative intelligence/sincerity.

4-9. Bergman, M. (1971). Changes in hearing with age. The Gerontologist, 11 (2, part 1), 148-151.

Hearing loss in older adults represents a major source of communication difficulties. In this essay, Bergman reviews the literature on this topic and notes that interference caused by competing noise and auditory interference in daily life can severely limit audition for older people.   In addition, so-called acceptable distortion in telephonic and radio transmission requires reevaluation.

4-10.   Bettinghaus, C. O., & Bettinghaus, E. P.   (1976).   Communication considerations in the health care of the aging.   In H. J. Oyer, & E. J. Oyer (Eds.) Aging and communication (pp. 129-154).   Baltimore, MD: University Park Press.

The relationship between older adults, and communication and health care fall into 3 major areas: (1) physiological changes (vision, hearing, mobility); (2) changes in personal living arrangements; and (3) social psychological theories that may relate to health care delivery, and the older person. Since older people are more likely to use health care services, it is important that this channel of communication be explored in depth.

4-11.   Blazer, D. (1971, November).   Techniques for communicating with your elderly patient. Geriatrics, 33, 79-84.

Because of the increase in older adults, it is likely that physicians and internists will have ever-increasing contact with geriatric patients. In this article, Blazer suggests strategies for improving communication with this segment of the patient population. There are patient factors (loss of reactions, life review, fear of loss of control), and physician factors (fear of death and aging) involved in the doctor-client communication. Suggestions for effective communication include the following: (1) respect the older patient; (2) speak clearly and slowly; (3) conduct a systematic inquiry into the patient's condition; (4) interview the patient at an even pace; and (5) assess the patient's situation realistically yet hopefully.

4-12.   Bloom, S. W., & Speedling, E. J.   (1981).   Strategies of power and dependence in doctor-patient exchanges.   In M. R. Haug (Ed.) Elderly patients and their doctors (pp. 157-170).   New York: Spring Publishing Company.

Effective patient-physician communication is extremely important for proper health-care management. The encounter of older adult patient and doctor often produces ambiguous role situations.   In this essay, Bloom and Speedling describe the sociological framework of superordinancy and subordination in a doctor-patient exchange. The older patient has been socialized in an earlier time period when the prevailing set of values including individualism, self-reliance, and other factors may no longer fit into the present social scheme. Recognition of these factors is crucial to effective communication between doctor and older patient.

4-13.   Boden, D., & Bielby, D. D.   (1983).   The past as resource: A conversational analysis of elderly talk.   Human Development, 26, 308-319.

An analysis of the conversation was employed to determine the importance of life history in the lives of older adults.   Data for this study derives from 2 sources: (1) a 36-minute dyadic conversation between 3 sets of males and females over the age of 62; and (2) a set of comparison data from 15 similar dyadic conversations with young adults enrolled in a first-year sociology course. The results indicate that conversations in both groups are similarly structured. However, the older people use the past to provide a meaning for the present which provides a shared sense of meaning.   This feature is lacking in the speech of the college students.

4-14.   Boden, D., & Bielby, D. D.   (1986).   The way it was: Topical organization in elderly conversation.   Language & Communication, 6, 73-89.

In this empirical study of the ways in which older adults structure the topics of their conversations, Boden and Bielby note that older speakers tend to use the past as a reference for the present.   Among the allusions to the past are name references, particular place name references, routine personal activities, and references to how life used to be.   The authors point out that much more research is needed in this new area of social communication with special attention to intergenerational, and inter-gender communicative situations.

4-15.   Bollinger, R. L.   (1974).   Geriatric speech pathology.   The Gerontologist, 14, 217-220.

Communication disorders constitute an important problem for geriatric patients, 45 to 50% of whom suffer from language/speech, and hearing disabilities. Since most of these disfluencies result from age-related maladies (arteriosclerosis, senile brain damage), it is necessary to assist afflicted patients to adjust to this situation, and to enhance the intact modalities.

4-16.   Butler, R. N.   (1979).   Breaking images: The media and aging. Columbia Journalism Monographs, 3, 37-45.

In this overview essay on the depiction of aging in the media, Butler discusses the relationship between stereotypes about old age, and its realities.   Suggestions to the press about acting to provide positive coverage are offered.   Finally, a "state of the art" review of research on aging follows.

4-17. Caporael, L. R. (1981). The paralanguage of care giving: Baby talk to the institutionalized aged. Journal of Personality and Social Psychology, 40, 876-884.

In this empirical analysis of the speech of caregivers in a health care facility licensed for 49 beds, tape recordings were made of conversations between health care providers and patients. A single health care provider per day was recorded, and each of these was recorded twice. 1,995 complete sentences were recorded, and participating judges then assessed these utterances. Results showed that baby talk (defined by its prosodic features of high pitch, and high pitch variability) is used to convey affection and nurturance. A total of three speech patterns (baby talk, non-baby talk, and adult speech) were rated on the basis of 4 criteria (comfort, pleasantness, irritation, arousal). Baby talk was rated as positive, adult speech had intermediate ratings, and non-baby talk was ranked negative. The latter was considered an institutional register designed to promote dependency.

4-18. Caporael, L. R., Lukaszewski, M. P., & Culbertson, G. H. (1983). Secondary baby talk: Judgments by institutional elderly and their caregivers. Journal of Personality and Social Psychology, 44, 746-754.

In this empirical analysis of nursing home speech, 3 registers were documented: (1) baby talk speech (high pitch and pitch variability) directed to older adult patients; (2) non-baby talk speech directed at other nursing home staff; and (3) normal adult talk. Results of his study indicate that the speech pattern used by nursing home personnel may be a result of expectations of older adults in general while positive reception of this form of speech corresponds to the older patient's functional status. The authors hypothesize that caregiver expectations concerning speech usage is a product of social stereotypes of older people.

4-19. Cassata, M. B. (1968). A study of the mass communications behavior and social disengagement behavior of 177 members of the age center of New England (Doctoral dissertation, Indiana University, Bloomington, 1967). Dissertation Abstracts, 28, 3765-A-3766-A.

The disengagement theory of aging by which an older person comes to terms with loss (death of a spouse, income, health, etc.) forms the theoretical foundation of this study. Cassata wanted to determine if the use of the mass media played a role in the disengagement process. The author found no outstanding relationships between her indices of disengagement and mass media usage. Nevertheless, the study yielded a great deal of information on the mass media usage habits of older adults which is to be found in the appendices of this dissertation.

4-20. Cohen, G., & Faulkner, D. (1986). Does 'elderspeak' work? The effect of intonation and stress on comprehension and recall of spoken discourse in old age. Language & Communication, 6, 91-98.

The authors observe that people who communicate with older people alter their speech. Specific manifestations include word stress to emphasize important meanings. In this experiment, 2 groups of 30 participants with 15 males, and 15 females each took part. The first group contained people from ages 62 to 80, the second had people aged 19-33. Passages from newspapers were read to the subjects with focal stress, and without focal stress. Subsequent to the reading of the text, the participants were asked content questions about the materials read. Results indicated that recall was aided by the use of heavy stress on certain key words. Little effect, however, was noticed with the younger group.

4-21. Coupland, N., Coupland, J., Giles, H., & Henwood, K. (1988). Accommodating the elderly: Invoking and extending a theory. Language in Society, 17, 1-41.

This outstanding scholarly article on intergenerational communication reviews the sociolinguistic literature on younger-older and older-younger communication. The authors point out ageist and stereotypic issues related to their research on intergenerational speech. Much remains to be done in this under-explored realm of sociolinguistics.

4-22. Coupland, N., Coupland, J., & Giles, H. (1991). Language, society, and the elderly: Discourse, identity, and aging. Oxford, England/Cambridge, MA: Blackwell.

This book treats various facets of communication of older adults. After an excellent literature review of language and later life, the authors discuss theories of discourse, accommodation, and intergenerational relations. Most of this text deals with an analysis of actual conversations with an older person in which the person engages in self-disclosure, and discussion of particular problems. The authors seek to determine how conversation contributes to the marginalization of older people in society. This excellent volume has implications for communication with older adults by health-care professionals, and others who deal with older adults. Another important facet of this book is that it consolidates, and synthesizes the authors' important previous research into a single, accessible volume.

4-23. Culbertson, G. J., & Caporael, L. R. (1983). Baby talk speech to the elderly: Complexity and content of messages. Personality and Social Psychology Bulletin, 9, 305-312.

A content analysis of baby talk directed to institutionalized older adults derived from tape-recorded conversations between health care providers and geriatric patients in a nursing home facility. Messages were categorized according to 7 types: offering, encouragement, imperative, sympathy, greeting, repeats, and other. Baby talk was defined by its characteristic high and variable pitch, as well as simplified semantic content. Non-baby talk was perceived as a form of intrusion that fostered institutional dependency.

4-24. Danowksi, J. (1976). Communication specialists in aging-related organizations. In H. J. Oyer, & E. J. Oyer (Eds.) Aging and communication (pp. 275-288). Baltimore, MD: University Park Press.

In this essay, Danowski examines organizations that specialize in aging from an information processing perspective. Theoretical in his approach, the author describes an effective model for an organization that focuses on the needs of older adults.

4-25. Farrell, M. T. (1976). Special living arrangements for the aging: The importance of communications. In H. J. Oyer & E. J. Oyer (Eds.) Aging and communication (pp. 253-273). Baltimore, MD: University Park Press.

Some older adults require specialized living environments often for medical reasons. In this essay, the author describes 6 living arrangements for older adults: (1) independent living (husband and wife); (2) independent living (widow/widower); (3) independent living (children or next of kin); (4) independent congregate living; (5) dependent congregate living; and (6) dependent health care living. Each type of living environment contains a set of questions to facilitate decision-making. Because of the significance of living arrangements, good and effective communication is absolutely necessary. A very useful listing of resources (dental-medical facilities, libraries, shopping, etc.) related to changes in living arrangements is included.

4-26. Haak, L. A. (1976). A retiree's perspective on communication. In H. J. Oyer, & E. J. Oyer (Eds.) Aging and communication (pp. 17-41). Baltimore, MD: University Park Press.

Written from the perspective of a retired person, this essay focuses on 4 topics: (1) who engages in communication; (2) what information is transmitted; (3) the symbols of communication; and (4) the procedures employed in transferring the symbols. A number of topics related to the communication needs of older adults are discussed (ethics, equality, language, lifestyles, adequacy of information). Haak ends his work by enumerating a list of research questions, possible future trends, and recommendations for facilitating communication among older adults.

4-27. Hess, B. B. (1974). Stereotypes of the aged. Journal of Communication, 24, 88-96.

In her previous thorough literature review, Hess found that many negative stereotypes of older adults were unfounded. This review essay focuses on a model of the mass communication media which views the vantage points of sender and receiver of the message with special attention to the older adult. Hess hopes that her collaborative research on the topic aging will advance a more accurate view of the older person and the process of aging.

4-28. Hutchinson, J. M., & Beasley, D. S. (1976). Speech and language functioning among the aging. In H. J. Oyer, & E. J. Oyer (Eds.) Aging and communication (pp. 155-174). Baltimore, MD: University Park Press.

The authors observe that the interpersonal communication possibilities of older adults are reduced because of the death of friends and acquaintances, and the mobility of family members. Moreover, deterioration in oral linguistic skills (disturbances in ideation, translation, and symbolization) due to the normal aging process may contribute to reduction in the development of new social contacts. Finally, communication disorders arising from neurological dysfunction is an additional source of communication loss.

4-29. Kaiser, S. B., & Chandler, J. L. (1984). Fashion alienation: Older adults and the mass media. International Journal of Aging and Human Development, 19, 203-221.

A total of 209 people over 50 completed a self-administered questionnaire concerning fashion alienation. Fashion alienation was determined by questions related to identification with fashion symbols in the media, and by social or economic disaffection from fashion. Results showed that the respondents were basically favorable toward media communication of fashion symbols. Nevertheless, the participants indicated no identification with the cultural icons in television fashion commercials. This study has implications concerning clothing-related stereotypes about aging.

4-30. Kynette, D., & Kemper, S. (1986). Aging and the loss of grammatical forms: A cross-sectional study of language performance. Language & Communication, 6, 65-72.

The authors note that geriatric psycholinguistic research is scarce. In this particular research project, 32 native speakers of English (ages 50-90) were divided into 4 age groups (50-59, 60-69, 70-79, and 80-89) with 4 men and 4 women in each group. Every adult produced a 20 minute speech sample. From this data base, speech errors were identified. Subsequently, 50 examples from each person was selected and submitted to the LINGQUEST analytical program. The results indicate that age correlates significantly with the types of structures used, percentage of correctly used structures, different tenses employed, and number of grammatical forms correctly used. This research has implications for both production and comprehension of speech by the "old old."

4-31. Kreps, G. (1986). Health communication and the elderly. World Communication, 15, 55-70.

Effective health care communication education is essential to the well-being of older consumers of health care services.   Such education needs to include appropriate programs for the health care providers, as well as consumers, involving older patients in the decision-making process, and the provision of consumer protection and information for the older patient.

4-32. Lubinski, R. B. (1978-1979). Why so little interest in whether or not old people talk: A review of recent research on verbal communication among the elderly. International Journal of Aging and Human Development, 9, 237-245.

This research review treats the role of communication from the perspective of the staff and the patient.   The role of communication is a fundamental determinant of the social interaction and mental health of an older person. Appropriate communication is a diagnostic tool for determining the notions of isolation, integration, and adjustment. Lubinski argues for more research in this area because of the relative paucity of available information.

4-33. Mauldin, C. R. (1976). Communication and the aging consumer. In H. J. Oyer, & E. J. Oyer (Eds.) Aging and communication (pp. 119-128). Baltimore, MD: University Park Press.

Certain key factors play a role in consumption by the older adults, namely, income, mobility, physical capacity, and changes in living environment. Additional research on the aged consumer, and the development of theoretical models for dealing with problems related to consumer behavior are necessary.

4-34. Millar-Davis, J. (1984). Normal and impaired speech in the elderly. Papers in Linguistics, 17, 89-111.

Millar-Davis notes that little research has been carried out on linguistic changes that occur in the speech of "normal" older adults but she provides a brief review of the available literature (syntax, semantics, phonology, pragmatics). The rest of this chapter deals with language in older adults suffering from dementia. Characteristics of language deterioration in older people includes fluent but meaningless speech. While disintegration of speech is progressive, the semantic components suffer at an early stage.

4-35. Muth, T. A. (1976). Legal and public policy problems in communication arising with aging. In H. J. Oyer, & E. J. Oyer (Eds.) Aging and communication (pp. 205-223). Baltimore, MD: University Park Press.

Law and public policy play an important role in the realm of aging and communication: (1) the implementation of communication for individual and group needs; (2) improvement of negative attitudes toward older people; (3) the promotion of accuracy about aging; and (4) consideration of the design and method of communication from older person to the larger society and vice-versa. Recommendations for implementation of policy issues include: (1) the sponsorship of appropriate legislation; (2) programs to support these rights; and (3) the special communication needs of older adults involved in the legal system.

4-36. Nuessel, F. (1988). Review of Communication and cognition in normal aging and dementia by K. A. Bayles, & A. W. Kaszniak, Boston: Little, Brown and Company. Language Problems and Language Planning, 12, 59-61.

A positive review of this book was based on its in-depth research, comprehensible prose, and organization. A generally agreed upon description of symptomatologies of speech disinfluences, however, continues to be an elusive goal. See 4-6.

4-37. Oyer, E. J. (1976). Exchanging information within the older family. In H. J. Oyer & E. J. Oyer (Eds.) Aging and communication (pp. 43-61). Baltimore, MD: University Park Press.

An account of communication in the older family has received little attention. Among the issues discussed include the barriers to family communication (generation gap, changes in residence, conflicts in values), the content of older adult communication (food, health, morale). Finally, a set of recommendations for additional research: (1) longitudinal studies; (2) younger family members need to learn active listening; (3) communication about housing; and (4) the use of cable television as a source of information about issues related to aging.

4-38. Oyer, E. J. (1976). Summary. In H. J. Oyer, & E. J. Oyer (Eds.) Aging and communication (pp. 289-297). Baltimore, MD: University Park Press.

In her overview of this volume, Oyer provides an excellent summary of the basic areas covered in this anthology. It may be wise to read this part of the book first before individual chapters. Appropriate communication with older adults is extremely important, and the studies in this volume provide sound recommendations in many of the relevant areas that affect older people on a continuing basis. Oyer echoes the sentiment of all of the contributors to this volume that more research in this area is needed.

4-39. Oyer, H. J., & Oyer, E. J. (Eds.) (1976). Aging and communication. Baltimore, MD: University Park Press.

The 17 chapters of this anthology deal with a wide variety of communication patterns and strategies involving older adults, e.g., family communication, intergenerational communication, communication networks, mass media, consumer information, health care, speech and language functions, hearing disorders, education, the law, organized religion, professional communication, living arrangements, and communication specialists. Each chapter follows a consistent format: (1) an overview of previous research; (2) suggestions for future research, (3) a summary of the main points; and (4) recommendations for dealing with specific issues raised in the chapter. Many of the issues discussed continue to be relevant today.

4-40. Oyer, H. J., & Oyer, E. J. (1976). Communicating with older people: Basic considerations. In H. J. Oyer, & E. J. Oyer (Eds.), Aging and communication (pp. 1-16). Baltimore, MD: University Park Press.

In this overview chapter on the relationship of the discipline of communication and aging, the editors define the term communication as verbal and non-verbal communicative acts with self or others. The communicative situations to be discussed in this book include: (1) individual communication; (2) small group communication; (3) large group communication; and (4) mass media communication. Among the topics worthy of discussion in the domain of aging and communication include the following: (1) attitudes; (2) significance of communication with older people; (3) communication as a problem, barriers to communication; (4) theoretical approaches to the study of aging; (5) unanswered research issues.

4-41. Oyer, H. J., Kapur, Y. P., & Deal, L. V. (1976). Hearing disorders in the aging: Effects upon communication. In H. J. Oyer, & E. J. Oyer (Eds.) Aging and communication (pp. 175-186). Baltimore, MD: University Park press.

Hearing impairment constitutes one of the most serious sensory losses for older adults. This problem has an immediate, negative effect on aural-oral communication. The most common forms of rehabilitation for older people who suffer from hearing loss include hearing aids, lipreading, auditory training, and counseling, or some combination thereof.

4-42. Ptacek, P. H. & Sander, E. K. (1966). Age recognition from voice. Journal of Speech and Hearing Research, 9, 273-277.

To ascertain the ability of people to distinguish older from younger voices, Ptacek and Sander carried out an experiment in which 10 graduate students were asked to identify a young person's voice (under 35) and an older person's voice (over 65). Three listening samples were presented in order of relative difficulty: (1) a prolonged vowel; (2) a reading sample played in reverse; and (3) a reading sample played normally (forward). Results indicate that the participants were uncanny in their ability to make this distinction in each situation.

4-43. Ramig, L. A. (1986). Aging speech: Physiological and sociological aspects. Language & Communication, 6, 25-34.

The author notes that people can usually identify a person's age on the basis of speech. The speech of older people has certain identifying characteristics. These features include: (1) aspects of sustained vowel phonation (hoarseness, breathiness); (2) traits of connected speech (slowness, long pauses, hesitancy); and (3) acoustic analysis of speech (increased silent time, longer pauses, increased duration of phonation). This experiment was designed to determine if identification of a speaker's age would correspond to speech mechanism degeneration. In this experiment, 30 males subdivided into 3 age categories (25-35, 45-55, 65-75). The physical health of the speakers was determined by resting heart beat, blood pressure, percentage of fat, and other factors. A total of 60 listeners participated (58 males, 2 females). The type of stimulus (connected speech versus sustained vowel phonation) affected accuracy of age assessment. This study supports the notion that physical condition plays a role in the determination of age and speech.

4-44. Ryan, E. B., Giles, H., Bartolucci, G., & Henwood, K. (1986). Psycholinguistic and social psychological components of communication by and with the elderly. Language & Communication, 6, 1-24.

Language communication in later life involves a number of factors such as health, receptive and expressive communication, neurological impairment, and other elements. An analysis of communication encounters with older adults demonstrates the "communicative predicament of old age" (stereotypical expectations, diminished self-esteem, physical changes, reduced social interaction reinforcement of age-stereotyped behavior, etc.).

4-45. Schlossberg, N. K. (1982). Older adults and the media: An agenda for tomorrow. National Forum, 62, 21-23.

The media have the potential to help and to harm. In this brief discussion on the representation of older adults in the media, Schlossberg notes that the media distort older people and old age by various means (underrepresentation, more men than women, etc.). Suggestions for changing the situation include: (1) the creation of a national council on mass media; (2) use of media to stimulate mental health and education; and (3) dissemination of adult developmental stages to those who control the media.

4-46. Shipp, T., & Hollien, H. (1969). Perceptions of the aging male voice. Journal of Speech and Hearing Research, 12, 703-710.

The identification of age from voice samples was the purpose of this research project. 175 male voices were recorded by people with ages from 20-89. These recordings then formed the basis of an experiment in which judges were asked to indicate if the speaker was "young," "old," or "neither." The participants were highly successful in their identification of a person's age based on listening to a tape recording of a voice.

4-47. Staser, C. W., & Staser, H. T. (1976). Organized religion: Communication considerations. In H. J. Oyer, & E. J. Oyer (Eds.) Aging and communication (pp. 225-237). Baltimore, MD: University Park Press.

Organized religions play an important role in the lives of older adults by creating a sense of belonging, a social cohesion that strengthens the overall society. Communication strategies with older adults include mail, telephone, small groups, ministerial counseling and visitations, lay visitation, nursing home ministries, neighborhood groups, between churches, and programs that use church facilities. Additional research is required, however, to find new and effective means of enhancing communication.

4-48. Stewart, M. A., & Ryan, E. B. (1982). Attitudes toward younger and older adult speakers: Effects of varying speech rates. Journal of Language and Social Psychology, 1, 91-109.

In this experiment, 60 undergraduate students at Notre Dame University listened to tape recordings of 3 younger male speakers (20-22 years of age), and 3 older male speakers (60-65 years of age). The speakers spoke in 3 styles of speech--

fast, medium, and slow. Students were asked to perform 4 tasks: (1) to rate the speakers on the basis of 18 personality and social scales; (2) to rate the success of failure of the speaker; (3) to estimate the age of the speakers; and (4) to rate the voices. Results showed that older, and slower speakers were evaluated less favorably.

4-49. Trager, N. P. (1976). Available communication networks for the aged in the community. In H. J. Oyer, & E. J. Oyer (Eds.) Aging and communication (pp. 75-97). Baltimore, MD: University Park Press.

The assertion that many formal and informal sources of information for older adults is subjected to scrutiny and criticism. For one thing, the use of modern technologies unfamiliar to many older people reduces their effectiveness. Moreover, automated systems approaches dehumanize some services. Efforts toward 2-way communication is necessary. Likewise, the more effective use of television and radio as educational tools must take place. Finally, subsidization of postal services, and the telephonic media is required.

4-50. Weinstein, B. E., & Ventry, I. M. (1982). Hearing impairment and social isolation in the elderly. Journal of Speech and Hearing Research, 25, 593-599.

Hearing impairment is one of the most prevalent sensory deficits in older adults. In this study, 80 male veterans were selected for participation. Each person reported hearing loss around age 53. A hearing test (Hearing Measurement Scale) was administered to determine the amount of impairment involved. Subsequently, each person was administered a Comprehensive Assessment and Referral Evaluation to determine emotional, social and physical problems that might be afflicting the individual. Next a possible correlation between the Hearing Measure Scale and the Objective and Subjective Social Isolation Scale was determined. A high correlation existed between the Subjective Scale and Hearing Measurement Scale.

4-51. Woelfel, J. (1976). Communication across age levels. In H. J. Oyer, & E. J. Oyer (Eds.) Aging and communication (pp. 63-73). Baltimore, MD: University Park Press.

The communication systems of this society shape beliefs of the general population. Because of rapid changes in this network in the recent past, a reduction in the inter-age communication has taken place. Additional research is necessary to assess the impact of these communicative transformations on older people in this society.

5

MEDIA GUIDELINES

5-1. Gamse, D. N. (Project Manager). (1984). Truth about aging: Guidelines for accurate communications. Washington, DC: American Association of Retired Persons.

This pamphlet contains brief sections on health, economics, families, leisure, social roles, general characteristics, and vocabulary, and graphic materials. In each case, ageist and non-ageist/recommended ways of expressing published material in a non-stereotypical fashion are offered. A final section provides recommendations for making printed, and nonprint materials easier to read, see, and hear.

5-2. Guidelines for creating positive images of persons and groups. (1978). Chicago: Coronet Films.

This booklet includes a section on appropriate methods of depicting older adults. The suggestions include: (i) intergenerational contacts; (2) depiction of older people in vital roles; (3) the portrayal of older citizens in positive and credible situations. A summary of these recommendations may be found in R. H. Davis and J. A. Davis TV's image of the elderly: A practical guide for change (p. 57, see 21-14).

5-3. Mathiason, G. (1977, March-April). It's time for fair play. Perspective on Aging, 6, 17-22.

In this article, NCOA's first executive director suggests ways to avoid stereotypic portrayal of older adults in the media. Accuracy and fairness demand the avoidance of exaggeration of mental and physical problems, ageist humor, inactivity, and institutionalization. Suggestions for positive characterizations are offered. References to and photographs of television personalities appear in this essay. A summary of this material may be found in R. H. Davis, & J. A. Davis TV's image of the elderly: A practical guide for change (pp. 57-58, see 21-14).

5-4. Wisnieski, C. J., Star, S. L., & Hermann, C. (1979). Media guidelines for sexuality and aging. Mimeograph. 3 pp. [Available from C. J. Wisnieski, 348 Diamond Street, San Francisco, CA 94114.]

These guidelines contain an explicit list of appropriate and inappropriate materials with examples. These guidelines are reprinted in Davis, R. H., Television and the aging audience, Los Angeles, CA: University of Southern California Press, pp. 83-84 (see 21-11).

6

CHILDREN'S LITERATURE

6-1. Almerico, G. M., & Fillmer, T. (1988). Portrayal of older characters in children's magazines. Educational Gerontology, 14, 15-31.

11 children's magazines were selected in this empirical analysis. Of 101 magazines with 2,186 stories analyzed, 123 stories featured at least one older adult. Although overt ageism was not present in this sample, subtle forms existed such as underrepresentation of older characters compared to the actual population, and a failure to develop their personalities. Recommendations to editors, publishers, writers, illustrators, and educators are offered. An appendix contains a worthwhile "Checklist for Analysis of Older Characters in Children's Magazines."

6-2. Ansello, E. F. (1976a). Ageism in picture books, part I: How older people are stereotyped. Interracial Books for Children Bulletin, 7, 4-6.

The data base for this study were the books in the Montgomery County (Maryland) Public Library system catalogued under the rubric "Easy and Juvenile Picture Books." In this preliminary essay, the author reported on 549 children's books with 225,000 pages and 18,000 graphics. Elements recorded in this empirical analysis included publication date, presence, sex, race, and behavior, physical description and personality traits of older adults, interaction of older adult with protagonist, and associated illustrations. Ansello concluded that the books scrutinized were largely ageist.

6-3. Ansello, E. F. (1976b). Ageism in picture books, part II: The rocking chair syndrome in action. Interracial Books for Children Bulletin, 7, 7-10.

In this essay, the author provides specific examples of ageist illustrations and language in children's literature. The characters are generally passive or marginal. Ansello states that most older people in these tales are underdeveloped, and inactive. A few positively portrayed characters, however, are cited.

6-4. Ansello, E. F. (1976c). Ageism in picture books, part III: Old age as a concept. Interracial Books for Children Bulletin, 7, 6-8.

In this article, the author reports on his evaluation of 656 children's books with a total of 27,000 pages and 22,000 illustrations. In the books studied, only 16.46% of the characters are older adults. The majority of the older characters are white (65.52%), and male (55.17%). Stereotyping of older adults is achieved in 2 basic ways: (1) omission (old people are insignificant); and (2) failure to develop the few old people present in the literature.

6-5. Ansello, E. F. (1977). Age and ageism in children's first literature. Educational Gerontology, 2, 255-274.

This study represents the comprehensive report of the author's content analysis of 656 children's books (see 6-2--6-4). Absence versus presence, gender, race, occupation, behavior, physical and behavioral descriptions, and graphic depiction of older adults are evaluated. Inattention to character development of older people (when they actually appeared) characterizes most children's literature.

6-6. Ansello, E. F. (1978). Ageism--the subtle stereotype. Childhood Education, 54(3), 118-122.

In this essay, the author again reviews the findings of his major study (see 6-2-6-4). Ansello advises teachers to become aware of the practice of ageism in order to combat such stereotypes in the academic environment.

6-7. Ansello, E. F. (1989). Children's first literature and the feast of life. The Gerontologist, 29, 272-277.

In this review essay, Ansello addresses the function of children's literature and its effect on children's attitudes toward older people. The author reviews 34 recent children's literature (since 1983), although he notes that this sample is a minuscule amount compared to the thousands of titles available. The author notes that the titles annotated in this article depict older people who are diverse, better developed, and more central.

6-8. Barnum, P. W. (1977a). The aged in young children's literature. Language Arts, 54(1), 29-32.

A selective survey of children's books based on the author's research (see 6-9), Barnum notes that older people and old age are depicted in negative fashion. The effect of such grim verbal and visual images is to propagate ageist stereotypes about old age and older people.

6-9. Barnum, P. W. (1977b). Discrimination against the aged in children's literature. The Elementary School Journal, 77(4), 301-306.

In a random sample of 100 children's books selected from books listed in the reference work Children's Catalogue (5 each year from 1950-1959 and 1965-1974), the author assessed 3 factors: (1) number of older people in texts and graphic materials; (2) social involvement; and (3) behavioral characteristics. Findings of the study based on a quantitative analysis revealed older adults were insignificant, and had a difficult life. The author speculates on the impact of this literature on attitude formation in children.

6-10. Blue, G. F. 1978. The aging as portrayed in realistic fiction for children 1945-1975. The Gerontologist, 18, 187-192.

125 books (including picture books) of realistic fiction published from 1945 to 1975, and known to feature at least one older character were surveyed. The author sought to ascertain eight elements (demography, physical aspects, health, personality, situation, activity, concept of age, and social intercourse) of older adults depicted in the books. Results of this study indicate that older persons were not stereotyped.

6-11. Butler, F. (1987). Portraits of old people in children's literature. The Lion and the Unicorn, 2, 26-37.

In this personal survey of children's tales, the author comments on selected literary works (most of recent vintage) which feature older adults. The observations in this essay are not based on empirical research, rather the evaluations are based on the author's reading of a large number of books. The books present both positive and negative views of aging and older adults.

6-12. Constant, H. (1977). The image of grandparents in children's literature. Language Arts, 54(1), 33-40.

In this selective examination of 17 children's books with grandparents, the author notes that grandparents are depicted in a variety of roles. Some are stereotypic while others are not. A wide variety of grandparental roles occur.

6-13. Fillmer, H. T., & Meadows, R. (1986). The portrayal of older characters in five sets of basal readers. Elementary School Journal, 86(5), 651-662.

A checklist (located in an appendix) of 13 categories (nationality, role, appearance, personality, etc.) and numerous subcategories was employed to evaluate older characters portrayed (553 in this sample) in 5 sets of basal readers. The results of the inquiry showed that some improvement in the depiction of older adults has taken place since the publication of earlier studies. Nevertheless, older characters do not reflect demographic reality in gender and race, marital status, and actual percentage of older people in the population. Implications of this study include suggestions for recognizing ageism, introduction of intergenerational programs, materials acquisition, and future research.

6-14. Janelli, L. M. (1988). The depiction of grandparents in children's literature. Educational Gerontology, 14, 193-202.

73 books about grandparents (42 about grandmothers 1961-1983 and 31 about grandfathers 1965-1984) formed the data base for this study. The author found that grandfathers and grandmothers were depicted stereotypically. Nevertheless, the former enjoyed a wider range of roles, and were more productive than the latter. Grandparents depicted in the sample were remarkably similar which rails to reflect the real diversity of older adults.

6-15. Katz, C. (1978). Outcasts and renegades: Elderly people in current children's fiction. Horn Book Magazine, 54, 316-321.

In this personal reaction to an unidentified article in The Gerontologist, the author bemoans the fact that such studies analyze children's literature from a social scientific rather than a literary perspective. Several children's books are then reviewed.

6-16. Kingston, A., & Drotter, W. (1981). The depiction of old age in six basal readers. Educational Gerontology, 6, 29-34.

A review of basal readers published by 6 major textbook companies for grades 1 through 6 revealed the appearance of 188 older adults. Statistical analysis showed 23.94% (N = 45) were grandmothers; 18.62% (N = 35) were grandfathers; while the rest represented other relatives or neighbors. Associated graphic art was non-realistic and depicted older adults in a stereotypic fashion. The author concludes that the readers examined treat older adults as insignificant and in an unrealistic manner.

6-17. Meadows, R. E. (1986). The portrayal of older adults in basal reading textbooks of the 1960s and 1980s (Doctoral Dissertation, University of Florida, 1986). Dissertation Abstracts International, 47, 1673A-1674A.

In this content analysis of basal reading textbooks, the author seeks the answers to 2 basic questions: (1) how are older adults portrayed in 5 sets of basal readers from the 1960s and the 1980s; and (2) what significant changes have occurred in their depiction? Answers to 21 additional information categories are also sought. Among the author's results, this study indicated that no biased portrayal existed in either set of readers, although older adults were underrepresented relative to their actual numbers in the population.

6-18. Meadows, R. E., & Fillmer, H. T. (1987). Depictions of aging in basal readers of the 1960s and 1980s. Educational Gerontology, 13, 85-100.

A comparison of 5 complete sets of basal readers from the 1960s and the 1980s. In the 2 periods, older adults were underrepresented by approximately half in terms of their statistical representation in the population. By the 1980s the number of older women increased by 12%. Basal readers depicted older adults in a variety of roles with generally positive personality traits. Positive characterization of older people occurred in 88% of the 1960s readers and 91% of those from the 1980s. Recommendations for editors, publishers, writers, teachers, and researchers are included. An appendix contains a checklist for analyzing older people.

6-19. Pearson-Davis, S. (1981). Images of old age in selected scripts for the young audience. Children's Theatre Review, 32(2), 3-6.

A selection of 35 plays for children was examined quantitatively to ascertain their depiction of old age. 11.5% of the characters were old (53 of 460). An analysis of biological, physical traits, physical trait value was carried out and revealed a gender distribution of 45% male and 55% female. Physical traits were negative (62%) and dominant dispositional characteristics were also negative (53%). Noteworthy was the fact that older females had more negative traits than males.   The author comments on the potential of plays to shape children's attitudes toward older people.

6-20.   Ribovich, J. K., & Deay, A. M.   (1979).   Portrayal of the elderly in basal readers.   Reading Psychology, 1, 32-40.

A total of 6 children's readers published from 1976 to 1978 were scrutinized in this study of the portrayal of older adults.   Although 16% of the characters were older adults, only 6% had major roles in the texts.   These researchers found that a qualitative assessment of the characteristics of older characters failed to show stereotypes of frailty, infirmity, dependence, and meaningless behavior and activity.   Graphic depictions of older adults, however, revealed traditional stereotypes.   The authors argue that text producers have become more sensitive to the depiction of older adults in their products.

6-21.   Robin, E. P.   (1977).   Old age in elementary school readers. Educational Gerontology, 2, 275-292.

In this empirical analysis, 4 sets of elementary school readers were compared. 3 sets were used in the Grand Rapids, Michigan public school system in 1970-1971 (these 47 readers were published from 1953 to 1968).   A fourth set of 33 was published in 1975.   The first group (1953-1968) of readers had 253 older adults while the second group (1975) contained 100 characters.   Older males outnumber older females by a ratio of 2:1 in the first group and 2.5:1 in the second.   Further comparison of the two groups of readers shows that number of older people is about the same (5.6% versus 5%).   In both sets, older people are positively depicted verbally and graphically though older persons generally lack vivid and memorable descriptors.   The author speculates about the effect of these readers on attitude formation in children.

6-22.   Rutherford, W. M.   (1981).   An exploratory study of ageism in children's literature (Doctoral dissertation, University of the Pacific, 1981). Dissertation Abstracts International, 42, 1938A-1939A.

A total of 80 fictional books for children published in the U.S. from 1949-1978 were reviewed for this study.   Rutherford scrutinized these texts for 3 basic elements: (1) the stereotypic portrayal of older adults; (2) measurement of the frequency and nature of this material; and (3) analysis of the information as it applies to children in grades K-6.   Results of the survey showed that the older characters were not depicted stereotypically.   The author recommends future research which includes: (1) a study of literature for other age groups; (2) an examination of children's literature toward older adults and the effects of their reading in the formulation of these notions; (3) an assessment of how children develop attitudes toward older people; (4) a comparative analysis of other literary genres; and (5) a replication of her own study with an adult and a child rater.

6-23. Seefeldt, C., Galper, A., Serock, K., & Jantz, R. K. (1978). The coming of age in children's literature. Childhood Education, 54(3), 123-129.

In this overview of children's literature, the authors review works that combat stereotypes. Among the topics explored positively are relationships with grandparents, extension of older peoples roles, and contributions of older adults. Nevertheless, the stereotype of older people is as wise and authoritative. These researchers advocate programs that promote intergenerational contact to avoid the limitations imposed by merely reading about older adults.

6-24. Seltzer, M. M., & Atchley, R. C. (1971). The concept of old: Changing attitudes and stereotypes. The Gerontologist, 11, 226-230.

In a study of children's literature from 1870 to 1960, Seltzer and Atchley reviewed random samples at 30 year intervals (1870, 1900, 1930, 1960) by using the techniques of semantic differential, content analysis and frequency count. The results indicated that there was not an increasingly negative depiction of older adults from the earlier to the later periods. The authors point out that their research design may have affected the results. A suggestion for a replication of this study is made with special attention to comic books, television, advertising, and pre-retirement literature.

6-25. Serra, J. K., & Lamb, P. (1984). The elderly in basal readers. Reading Teacher, 38(3), 277-281.

4 sets of basal readers (Ginn, Houghton Mifflin, Scott, Foresman, and Heath American Readers) for grades 1 through 6 were examined. The study indicated that only 68% of the characters in 1,036 stories contained older adults, though 11.4% of the U.S. population is over 65. In those stories with older people, 6 basic patterns emerged: (1) close interpersonal contact; (2) older adults faced with problems and challenges; (3) interpersonal relationship of older adult and unrelated person; (4) older person as socially involved; (5) older person in non-stereotypic role; and (6) older adult as a source of wisdom. The authors believe that progress in avoidance of ageist stereotypes has taken place.

6-26. Stone, M. R. M. (1985). The effect of selected children's literature on children's attitudes toward the elderly (Doctoral dissertation, University of Alabama, 1985). Dissertation Abstracts International, 46, 3597A.

In this empirical analysis of the effect of children's literature on attitudes toward older adults, Stone used twenty-five books read aloud to children. One significant result was recorded. When children were read positive stories about older adults, their attitudes toward this group improved measurably.

6-27. Storck, P. A., & Cutler, M. B. (1977). Pictorial representation of aging. Educational Gerontology, 2, 293-300.

A content analysis of 123 fiction and non-fiction books for children from an original total of 166 (37 children's books that won the Caldecott Medal and 129 runners-up) was conducted. Since 43 books contained no adults, they were excluded from this assessment. A total of 751 adults was identified. Results of the research led to 4 conclusions: (1) there were more men than women; (2) more healthy as opposed to physically challenged adults appeared; (3) more positive than negative depictions occurred; and (4) more adults appeared in fictional than in non-fictional works. The authors commented on the fact that these books do not reflect the reality of the world, e.g., male-female ratio, physically challenged people, etc.

6-28. Storey, D. C. (1977). Gray power: An endangered species? Ageism as portrayed in children's books. Social Education, 41, 528-533.

More than 100 children's books published between 1972 and 1977 were scrutinized, and many were found to be ageist because older adults are often stereotypic in their characterization of this age group. The author suggests ways to combat these practices by having children interview an older relative, and the selection of non-ageist reading materials. An appended annotated bibliography of juvenile literature featuring older characters positively and negatively is a useful resource.

6-29. Storey, D. C. (1979). Fifth graders meet elderly book characters. Language Arts, 56(4), 408-412.

In this report of a 5-week project carried out with fifth-grade children in Western Michigan, the author describes a study program about ageism. Several elements were included: (1) terminology and questions about aging; (2) preparations of questions for a grandparental interview; (3) discussion of older characters in children's books; (4) introduction of an older adult into the classroom setting; and (5) various guided activities. The author reports a positive reception to her unit on ageism with its combination of actual intergenerational contracts and academic projects.

6-30. Taylor, C. C. (1980). Images of the elderly in children's literature. Reading Teacher, 34(3), 344-347.

In this essay, the author reviews major studies on the appearance and depiction of older adults in children's literature.

6-31. Ventis, D. G. (1986). Humor and aging in children's books: Is the joke on grandpa? In L. Nahemow, K. A. McCluskey-Fawcett, & P. E. McGhee (Eds.), Humor and aging (pp. 223-231). Orlando, FL: Academic Press.

In a survey of 37 children's picture books, the raters evaluated the humorous content (positive-neutral-negative). 28 instances of humor were identified. Of the 23 characters involved, 43% were older adults. The author found that much of the humor involving older characters portrayed them as engaging in frivolous activity or acting in a ridiculous manner. The author suggests that future research should evaluate developmental differences in what is humorous. Likewise, other age groups should be studied.

6-32. Watson, J. J. (1981). A positive image of the elderly in literature for children. Reading Teacher, 34(7), 792-798.

Extant research reviewed by the author indicated that the depiction of older adults was largely negative. In this article, the author documents several examples of children's reading materials that portray older people in a positive fashion. Watson discusses how the books mentioned in this essay can be used to change certain stereotypic views, and to promote an appreciation of older people.

7

ADOLESCENT LITERATURE

7-1. Baggett, M. C. (1981). A study of the image of the senior adult in selected, recommended American fiction intended for adolescents, 1960-1978 (Doctoral dissertation, Mississippi State University, 1980). <u>Dissertation Abstracts International</u>, <u>41</u>, 3306A-3307A.

In this empirical analysis of 76 books recommended for adolescents, a 40 item checklist was used to determine the image of the older adult. Baggett found the following socioeconomic distribution: (1) professionals (21%); (2) upper-middle or middle income (19.66%); (3) in poverty (27%). Most older adults were depicted realistically in 21 of the 40 categories. Negative stereotyping occurred in 1 category (sex), and positive depictions were found in 10 additional domains. In the remaining categories, no majority was indicated. In the decade of the 70s, it is significant to note that the characterization of older people improved in 4 areas, while there was a deterioration in 15 other categories.

7-2. Baggett, C. (1982). Positive portraits of the elderly in realistic fiction for young adults. <u>Catholic Library World</u>, <u>54</u>, 60-63.

An evaluation of several contemporary novels for adolescents, Baggett shows that older adults can be portrayed in a realistic and non-patronizing fashion. The novels reviewed in this essay are: (1) Vera and Bill Cleaver, <u>The Queen of Hearts</u>; (2) Eth Clifford, <u>The Rocking Chair Rebellion</u>; (3) John Donovan,

Remove Protective Coating a Little at a Time; (4) Josh Greenfield and Paul Mazursky, Harry and Tonto; (5) Norma Fox Mazer, A Figure of Speech; (6) Gil Rabin, Changes; (7) Don Schellie, Kidnapping Mr. Tubbs; and (8) Barbara Wersba, The Dream Watcher.

7-3. Gerlach, J. (1988). Adolescent literature: A misrepresentation of youth-aged relationships. Educational Gerontology, 14, 183-191.

An analysis of the portrayal of older adults in 6 novels targeted at adolescents reveals unrealistic depictions of intergenerational contacts.   The literature sampled provides inaccurate information about encounters between older and young adults. Selection of literature for this age group requires care since it affects attitudes and shapes opinions.

7-4.   Peterson, D. A., & Eden, D. Z.   (1977).   Teenagers and aging: Adolescent literature as an attitude source. Educational Gerontology 2, 311-325.

53 books awarded the Newbery Medal for adolescent literature (1922-1975) were scrutinized for their portrayal of older adults. Results showed that older characters were not under-represented; however, they were underdeveloped and cast in marginal roles. The authors argue that greater development of older characters is necessary to avoid a continuation of the notion that older people are simple or insignificant.

7-5. Peterson, D. A., & Karnes, E. L. (1976). Older people in adolescent literature. The Gerontologist, 16, 225-231.

Winners of the Newbery Medal for adolescent literature (53 books) were analyzed for their portrayal of older adults. Results of this content analysis revealed that there were 159 older people (94 men and 65 women) in the sample (12% of all characters). The researchers state that the older characters in these books resemble older people in the contemporary U.S. because of their marginalized roles.

8

LITERATURE

ANTHOLOGIES OF LITERARY CRITICISM

8-1. Bagnell, v. D., P., & Soper, P. S. (Eds.). (1989). <u>Perceptions of aging in literature: A cross-cultural study</u>. New York: Greenwood Publishing Group.

In this volume there are 9 studies on national or language-specific literatures (Greek and Roman, British and American, French, German and Sutrain, Russian, Hispanic American, Arabic, Japanese, and Chinese). A foreword by W. Andrew Achenbaum, an overview essay, and a useful index complement this volume. The editors note that their anthology belongs to what many have come to designate "humanistic gerontology" which deals with "a portrait of aging in a cultural and historical perspective illuminated by diverse national literatures" (xxiii). Each chapter contains critical commentary on the literature and carefully selected examples in translation where the language is not English.

8-2. Falkner, T. M., & DeLuce, J. (Eds.). (1989). <u>Old age in Greek and Latin literature</u>. Albany, NY: State University of New York Press.

A total of 12 studies (including an introduction, an afterword and a bibliographic essay) are contained in this anthology. The meaning of old age in classical Greek and Latin poetry and dramatic literature is scrutinized. This collection of scholarly studies provides a sound overview of the classical perspective on aging and older people.

8-3.   Kenyon, G. M., Birren, J. E., & Schroots, J. J. F. (Eds.). (1991). Metaphors of aging in science and the humanities. New York: Springer Publishing Company.

A veritable explosion of interdisciplinary interest in metaphor as a figure of thought rather than a figure of speech is reflected in this collection of 12 essays on the metaphors related to aging employed in the sciences and the humanities. Each essay has its own bibliography. A name index and a subject index complement this volume.

8-4.   Porter, L., & Porter, L. M. (Eds.). (1984). Aging in literature. Troy, MI: International Book Publishers.

This anthology of essays on the theme of aging in various literary works (all cited and annotated in this chapter) contains a foreword by Robert N. Butler, an introduction on the aging and social responsibility, 9 critical essays (each with an insightful introduction by the editors), and a conclusion by Henri Peyre about the nature of age in literature. See 8-64.

8-5.   Spicker, S. F., Woodward, K. M., & Van Tassel, D. (Eds.). (1978). Aging and the elderly: Humanistic perspectives. Atlanta Highlands, NJ: Humanities Press.

This collection of analytical studies from a variety of humanistic perspectives contains a total of 18 chapters in 5 divisions: (1) The Western heritage: Images and Ideals; (2) Dementia, competency and senescent meditation; (3) Aging, death and destiny; (4) The polity and the elderly: Modernization, revolution and equity; and (5) Theoretical considerations. Those essays that treat literary subjects are annotated in this chapter. Introductory essays by Erik H. and Joan M. Erikson, and David E. Stannard, as well as afterward by Robert N. Butler complement this volume.

8-6.   Van Tassel, D. D. (Ed.). (1979). Aging, death, and the completion of being. Philadelphia: University of Pennsylvania Press.

This anthology features 3 parts: (1) Aging and death in contemporary society: Myths and realities; (2) Aging and death in the past: Attitudes and behavior; and (3) Aging and death as universal experience: Literary and artistic perceptions. Several of the eleven chapters are annotated in this book.

8-7. Woodward, K., & Schwartz, M. M. (Eds.). (1986). Memory and desire: Aging--literature--psychoanalysis. Bloomington, IN: Indiana University Press.

The 10 chapters in this anthology contain essays on various humanistic perspectives on aging (the relevant chapters are cited and annotated in this chapter). An introductory chapter by the Shakespearean scholar, Murray W. Schwartz, is included. See 8-38.

GENERAL

8-8. Achenbaum, W. A. (1989). Foreword: Literature's value in gerontological research. In P. von Dorotka Bagnell & P. Spencer Soper (Eds.), Perceptions of aging in literature: A cross-cultural study (pp. xiii-xxii). New York: Greenwood Press.

The emergence of a humanistic perspective on aging over the past 2 decades represents a novel dimension. Scholars in this tradition generally have 2 objectives: (1) to define and explicate the cross-cultural traditions and transformations of aging; and (2) to comprehend the social forces that play a role in the ideology of aging.

8-9. Achenbaum, W. A. (1990). Why the gerontological muses demur. The Gerontologist, 30, 276-279.

In this essay, 2 recent works on old age are reviewed critically (Old age in Greek and Latin literature edited by T. M. Falkner, and J. de Luce, New York: State University Press, 1989; and Old age in the old regime by D. G. Troyanksky, Ithaca, NY: Cornell University Press, 1989). Achenbaum observes that multidisciplinary research on aging depends on high quality scholarship in all academic areas including the humanities, and he argues for the stimulation of meaningful interdisciplinary interactions. See 8-2.

8-10. Achenbaum, W. A. (1991). 'Time is the messenger of the gods': A gerontologic metaphor. In G. M. Kenyon, J. E. Birren, & J. J. F. Schroots (Eds.), Metaphors of aging in science and the humanities (pp. 83-101). New York: Springer Publishing Company.

In a historical analysis of the basic metaphor "time is the messenger of the gods," Achenbaum reviews different disciplinary notions of the concept. This notion has several referents including objectivity and relativity, measurement, transformations, diversity, wisdom, and others. This metaphor, and its possible interpretations shape how disciplines view aging.

8-11.　Ansello, E. F. (1977).　Old age and literature:　An overview. Educational Gerontology, 2, 211-218.

Monotonic theories of aging, i.e., those which depict life-span development as an inevitable passage into a period of loss and deterioration are precisely those that coincide with historical views of old age.　An analysis of old age and literature supports the contention that the printed word mirrors culturally defined stereotypes about aging and older adults.　This essay focuses on several existing studies of different types of literature ranging from children's literature to the literary classics.　Ansello notes that children's literature, in particular, contains more ageist material than that devoted to other audiences.

8-12.　Beauvoir, S. de.　(1972).　The coming of age.　Trans. by P. O'Brian. New York:　Putnam.

Situating this monumental study of aging into any single category is virtually impossible.　De Beauvoir's work is included in literature because there are numerous references to literature throughout the volume.　The 8 lengthy chapters deal with anthropological, biological, sociological, historical, literary, artistic, ethical, and philosophical aspects of old age and older adults.　A reading of this monograph will provide the literary scholar with one of the most thorough references on these subjects available anywhere.　See 8-25.

8-13. Berman, L., & Sobkowska-Ashcroft, I. (1987). Images and impressions of old age in the great works of western literature (700 B.C.-1900 A.D.): An analytical compendium. Lewiston, Maine/Queenston:　St. David's University Press.

The data-base for these computer-generated indices of 267 "great" books (including the bible) by 87 or more authors derives from the Encyclopedia Britannica's Great Books of the Western World, and Gateway to the Great Books, as well as certain authors contained in Le Petit Larousse illustré.　The compilers include 6 basic indices (attitude of author, attributes, century, genre, nationality, and title of work).　The longest section of this book provides detailed information to each of the 267 references (bibliographic citation, additional information on the author, and additional information on the work). Finally, a list of the authors, a list of the books of the bible, and a list of anonymous works is included.　This reference provides an invaluable literary historical account of authors' attitudes (negative and positive) toward older adults in significant literature.

8-14. Berman, L., & Sobkowska-Ashcroft, I. (1986). The old in language and literature. Language and Communication, 6, 139-145.

This essay constitutes a research report on the computer-based project cited in 8-13 above.   The authors make the point that the linguistic and literary references to "old" may reveal much about attitudes toward older adults. This literature-based research indicates that writers from the same period have similar attitudes toward older people which suggests that cultural and social influences play a role in the development of attitudes.   Nevertheless, Berman and Subkowska-Ashcroft note the problems associated with attributing characteristics associated with older people derive from the process of aging itself, basic personality traits, or the conditions of a given society.

8-15. Birren, J. E., & Lanum, J. (1991). Metaphors of psychology and aging. In G. M. Kenyon, J. E. Birren, & J. J. F. Schroots (Eds.), Metaphors of aging in science and the humanities (pp. 103-129). New York: Springer Publishing Company.

The metaphors employed by psychologists to describe the relationship between aging and behavior is the subject of this essay.   An understanding of contemporary metaphors helps the researcher to see research paths.   Many current metaphors of aging are contradictory, e.g., aging as a set of deterministic stages of life versus a notion that the aging organisms enjoy a certain plasticity which allows for potential development.

8-16.   Blau, H. (1986).   The makeup of memory in the Winter of Our Discontent. In K. Woodward, & M. M. Schwartz (Eds.), Memory and desire: Aging--literature--psychoanalysis (pp. 13-36).   Bloomington, IN: Indiana University Press.

In this personal discussion about the relationship of memory to aging, Blau refers to numerous literary portrayals of aging to anchor his thoughts on this subject. This essay reflects the multiple problems and difficulties of growing old in our society.

8-17. Carp, L. (1955). Cicero speaks on old age. Geriatrics, 10, 43-45.

De senectute contains Cicero's thoughts about old age. The Roman philosopher specifies 4 difficulties of old age in this well known essay: (1) eliminates a person's ability to engage in world affairs; (2) development of physical ailments; (3) reduction of erotic activity; and (4) a portent of death. In the rest of his essay, Cicero refutes each one of these 4 points systematically. Carp argues that Cicero's vision of old age holds true today.

8-18.   Chandler, A. R. (1948).   Aristotle on mental aging.   Journal of Gerontology, 3, 220-224.

Aristotle commented upon mental aging in the second book of his Rhetoric. The famed Greek philosopher specified 15 distinctions between older and younger people. These differences include such traits as optimism and pessimism, isolation, loneliness, reduced sexuality, sense of inadequacy, and so forth. Chandler compares Aristotle's observations with those of contemporary psychologists and observes that Aristotle's writings on this topic anticipated, and supplemented modern psychology in many respects.

8-19.   Chandler, A. R.   (1948).   Cicero's ideal old man.   Journal of Gerontology, 3, 285-289.

In his well-known dialogue, De Senectute, Cicero wrote about old age. In this essay, Chandler compares Cicero's views on aging with those of Aristotle, and a contemporary psychologist. For Cicero, ideal old age includes physical activity and vigor, pleasant personality, community service, reduced sex drive, toleration of predictable age-based changes, a belief in immortality, and so forth. Chandler notes that Cicero anticipates, and is harmonious with modern psychological observations on aging.

8-20.   Chandler, A. R. (1949).   The traditional Chinese attitude towards old age.   Journal of Gerontology, 4, 239-244.

A review of Chinese literature shows a pattern of esteem for older people. In particular, the family structure creates an environment in which the children offer respect, security, and honor to their elders. Moreover, the wisdom of age derives from long life experience in a stable society. This model would be welcome in the west.

8-21.   Charles, D. C. (1977).   Literary old age: A browse through history. Educational Gerontology, 2, 237-253.

Any overview must, of necessity, be selective. Charles includes literature from the Bible, the "classics," and 19th and 20th century plays, poetry and novels as well as certain pieces of popular 20th century fiction. This author concludes that the notable absence of older people in literature and their negative depiction reflect their relative status in the "real world" during the last 2,500 years. 2 implications derive from this survey: (1) the need to recognize the literary and educational sources of our attitudes toward older adults and aging; and (2) to communicate this information to the members of the teaching profession to combat ageist viewpoints.

8-22.   Chinen, A. B. (1987).   Fairy tales and psychological development in late life: A cross-cultural hermeneutic study. The Gerontologist, 27, 340-346.

Fairy tales which feature older people are the subject of this essay on adult psychological development. Elder tales, according to Chinen, are unusual in Western Europe, though much more common in the Asian and Middle Eastern traditions. In this study, a mere 2% of 2,500 fairy tales featured older protagonists. Several themes were recurrent in these texts: (1) poverty; (2) self-reformation; (3) transcendence; (4) worldly wisdom; (5) emancipated innocence; and (6) mediation with the supernatural. Fairy tales with older characters symbolize lofty ideals. At the same time, however, these folkloristic texts provide interesting reading for a prototypical setting of grandparent and grandchild.

8-23. Coffman, G. R. (1934). Old age from Horace to Chaucer: Some literary affinities and adventures of an idea. Speculum, 9, 249-277.

According to Coffman, this study has 2 purposes: (1) to review the protean quality of descriptions of old age from the Latin writer Horace to certain medieval writers; and (2) to relate this information to certain transformations in Chaucer's writings on this subject. In this detailed examination of Horatian poetry and the works of certain medieval writers, the author finds important influences on Chaucer.

8-24. Coffman, G. R. (1937). Old age in Chaucer's day. Modern Language Notes, 52, 25-26.

In this brief note, Coffman poses the question of what constituted old age in Chaucer's time. The author refers to a poem from 1,350 which describes youth as 30 years, middle age as 60 years, and old age as 100 years.

8-25. Coles, R. (1972, August 19). Review of The coming of age. Trans. by P. O'Brian, New York: Putnam, 1972. The New Yorker, pp. 68, 71-74, 77-79.

In this critical review of Simone de Beauvoir's major treatise on old age, Coles observes that this depiction of aging is bleak. Only at the end of the work is there a positive note. The author of this review is unsympathetic to de Beauvoir's point of view which he attributes to the French writer's consistently anti-capitalist stance. See 8-12.

8-26. Covey, H. C. (1989). Old age portrayed by the ages-of-life models from the middle ages and the 16th century. The Gerontologist, 29, 692-698.

Written accounts and visual depictions of old age and older adults constitute the source material for Covey's study on developmental models of the life span.

Extant documents reveal that several themes pervade the ages-of-life models of the periods under review: (1) ambivalence; (2) physical degradation; (3) predictability of the stages of life; and (4) age-appropriate behavior.

8-27. Davidson, W. A. S. (1991). Metaphors of health and aging: Geriatrics as metaphor. In G. M. Kenyon, J. E. Birren, & J. J. F. Schroots (Eds.), Metaphors of aging in science and the humanities (pp. 173-184). New York: Springer Publishing Company.

The basic metaphors of health and aging focus on disease, decline,and deterioration. Since this type of figurative language prevails in geriatric medicine, the result is a prejudice in favor of younger medical consumers whose treatment will yield more positive and lasting results. The rejection of the traditional metaphoric medical view of aging will help to transform this treatment into a perspective which promotes healthy, and productive aging.

8-28. Deck, A. C. (1985). Depictions of elderly blacks in American literature. Explorations in Ethnic Studies, 8(2), 15-27.

Abundant and varied characterizations of older African-Americans exist in American literature. In this informative review of older Blacks in literary fiction, Deck notes that the depiction of this character depends largely upon the individual writer's attitudes toward African-Americans in general and older Blacks in particular. The portrayals include Joel Chandler Harris's nineteenth century stereotype of Uncle Remus, and William Faulkner's Dilsey in The Sound and the Fury. Other accounts portray older African-American men and women in a more positive and non-stereotypical light. (See also 8-55, 8-62, 8-73).

8-29. Dennefer, D. (1991). The race is to the swift: Images of collective aging. In G. M. Kenyon, J. E. Birren, & J. J. F. Schroots (Eds.), Metaphors of aging in science and the humanities (pp. 155-172). New York: Springer Publishing Company.

The view of aging as a collective phenomenon is the subject of this study. In particular, the current popularity of aging as a collective process, Dannefer, believes has a negative impact on individual lives. Through a process of age-grading, a member of a particular age cohort may receive beneficial or detrimental treatment according to the prevailing philosophy concerning older people.

8-30. DeSalvo, L. A. (1980). Literature and the process of aging. Media and Methods, 16(6), 22-23, 45-47.

Literature is an important resource for learning about aging. Several fictional works are cited (Muriel Spark's <u>Memento Mori</u>, Ernest Hemingway's <u>The Old Man and the Sea</u>) with specific references to the themes treated, especially, intergenerational contacts, and the necessity of facing death.

8-31. Donow, H. S. (1990-1991). The literature of aging and its place in the gerontology curriculum. <u>AGHExchange</u>, <u>14</u>(2), 1-3.

Donow sent a questionnaire to 59 gerontology programs to determine if there was a course on the "literature of aging." There were 21 responses with the following results: (1) 6 had a course on the literature of aging: (2) 5 had a course with a humanistic component; (3) 1 had both types of courses; and (4) 5 had no course. Several suggestions are made for the effective future implementation of such a course. The most important, of course, is to select appropriate literary examples. Gerontology programs, Donow argues, need a humanistic component in addition to the clinical dimension.

8-32. Edel, L. (1979). Portrait of the artist as an old man. In D. Van Tassel (Ed.), <u>Aging, death, and the completion of being</u> (pp. 193-214). Philadelphia: University of Pennsylvania Press.

Comparative scrutiny of 2 novelists (Leo Tolstoy, Henry James) and a poet (William Butler Yeats) provides Edel with evidence for his assertion that the final stage of an artist's life often provides the critic with the most important information for understanding the entire life of the person. According to the author, each one of these writers reached a period of triumph and fulfillment in his old age albeit in a very distinct way.

8-33. Fiedler, L. A. (1977) Eros or Thanatos: Or the mythic aetiology of the dirty old man. <u>Salgamundi</u>, <u>38-39</u>, 3-19.

In this excellent exploratory essay of the mythic character of the "dirty old man," Fiedler addresses the dichotomous tension between <u>eros</u> (sexual love) and <u>thanatos</u> (death) as portrayed in the literary works of writers such as Chaucer, Shakespeare, Thomas Mann, Balzac, and others. Several films are also cited, e.g., Bergman's <u>Wild Strawberries</u>, and <u>The Blue Angel</u>.

8-34. Fiedler, L. A. (1979). Eros and Thanatos: Old age in love. In D. Van Tassel (Ed.), <u>Aging, death, and the completion of being</u> (pp. 235-254). Philadelphia: University of Pennsylvania Press.

This is the same essay as the one cited in 8-33 above.

8-35. Fiedler, L. A. (1985). More images of Eros and old age: The damnation of Faust and the fountain of youth. In K. Woodward, & M. M. Schwartz (Eds.), Memory and desire: aging--literature--psychoanalysis (pp. 37-50). Bloomington, IN: Indiana University Press.

This essay constitutes an extension of Fiedler's earlier essay on the mythic nature of the "dirty old man." This time the author speaks of his own experiences as sexagenarian in an effort to arrive at a more personalized comprehension of the myth he is discussing. An examination of Goethe's Faust as well as many insightful references to the great literature with which Fiedler is intimately acquainted helps him to understand his own situation.

8-36. Finley, M. I. (1989). The elderly in classical antiquity. In T. M. Falkner & J. de Luce (Eds.), Old age in Greek and Latin literature (pp. 1-20). Albany, NY: State University of New York Press.

An accurate picture of older adults in classical antiquity is problematic at best. The dearth of information is formidable. Recorded history focuses largely on the financially secure and powerful men of the time. Finley's overview of older people deals with sociological, psychological and biological aspects of antiquity, albeit incomplete because of the lack of sufficient records. The author employs literature as a source of data about older people even though he recognizes its considerable drawbacks. The reader will find this essay to be quite enlightening.

8-37. Freedman, R. (1978). Sufficiently decayed: Gerontophobia in English literature. In S. F. Spicker, K. M. Woodward, & D. Van Tassel, Aging and the elderly: Humanistic perspectives in gerontology (pp. 49-61). Atlantic Highlands, NJ: Humanities Press, Inc.

Fear of aging as a theme in English literature is abundant. In this essay, Freedman provides a selective perspective of some rather negative literary views of aging. Among the writers cited are the following: Congreve (The Way of the World); Swift (Gulliver's Travels); Frances Burney (Evelina); Jane Austen (Sense and Sensibility); and Arnold Bennett (The Old Wive's Tale). This literature offers a generally unappealing portrayal of old age, yet its essential literary value can help the reader to appreciate the complexities of this stage of life.

8-38. Friedsam, H. J. (1987). Review of Memory and desire: Aging--literature--psychoanalysis ed. by K. Woodward and M. M. Schwartz, Bloomington, IN: Indiana University Press, 1986. The Gerontologist, 27, 253.

An extremely favorable account of the high quality of the essays in this anthology is offered by Friedsam. The application of the psychoanalytic theories of Freud, Erikson, and Lacan predominate in these studies. See 8-7.

8-39. Griffin, J. J. (1946). The Bible and old age. Journal of Gerontology, 1, 464-471.

According to Griffin, the Bible contains numerous allusions to old age. Many of the observations found there are comparable to those noted today. Negative references (failing health, skin texture, and other afflictions), and positive features (dignity, respect, and affection) are to be found in the Bible. An appendix of biblical references to old age is included.

8-40. Haynes, M. S. (1956). The concept of old age in the late middle ages with special reference to Chaucer (Doctoral dissertation, University of California, Los Angeles, 1956). Dissertation Abstracts, 16, 139.

The author seeks the roots of late medieval attitudes towards old age in Greek and Roman literature as well as in the Bible (chapters 1-3). The final 2 chapters examine aging in the English, French, Italian and Latin literature of the twelfth to fifteenth centuries, and in the work of Chaucer.

8-41. Haynes, M. S. (1963). The supposedly golden age for the aged in ancient Rome (a study of literary concept of old age). The Gerontologist, 3, 26-35.

Among the Roman writers featured in this overview are Cicero, Cato, Plautus, Terence, Horace, Seneca, and Pliny. Specific commentary on old age found in each of these writers is documented and discussed. Among the general findings by Haynes are the following: (1) realistic accounts of old age refer to physical decline and loss of mental acuity in this final stage of life; (2) older people were accorded great respect; (3) a small contingent of older adults enjoyed a comfortable life style; and (4) suicide was an acceptable option.

8-42. Hendricks, J., & Leedham, C. A. (1989). Making sense: Interpreting historical and cross-cultural literature on aging. In P. von Dorotka Bagnell & P. Spencer Soper (Eds.), Perceptions of Aging in Literature: A Cross-Cultural Study (pp. 1-16). New York: Greenwood Press.

Although aging is universal, its significance and perception are determined by culture, social structure, and economic factors. International literature provide a source of data for a determination of the specific cultural meaning of old age. A judicious interpretation of old age in a cross-cultural perspective requires the assessment of a number of factors including literary convention, culture, the time frame within which a work is written, as well as authorial intention.

8-43. Hilker, M. A. (1991). Generational viewpoints in culturally diverse literature: Commentary. International Journal of Aging and Human Development, 33, 211-215.

In her commentary on a special section on aging in literature in this journal, Hilker addresses the role of women in the different cultures represented. Ethnic literature of aging depicts intergenerational conflict and harmony. In each instance, the woman maintains and transmits culture.

8-44. Kastenbaum, R. (1989). Old men created by young artists: Time-transcendence in Tennyson and Picasso. International Journal of Aging and Human Development, 28, 81-104.

In this study, Kastenbaum raises questions about the relationship of a youthful creation of a distinctive older character, and its subsequent effect on the artist in later life. The poet Alfred Lord Tennyson, and artist Pablo Picasso are two creative individuals who worked in different media, yet both experienced the death of a close friend at an early age. This event inspired each artist to create a distinctive older protagonist, Tennyson's Ulysses, and Picasso's The Old Guitarist. The author concludes that each artist used this experience in different ways. For Picasso, it was a denial of death, while for Tennyson, the experience served as a constant reminder of a lurking death. The creation of a future self may, in fact, be a more general phenomenon which merits further study.

8-45. Keating, G. C. Fashionable pride: An ageless concern. International Journal of Aging and Human Development, 33, 187-196.

Due to the Civil War which left many young men dead, a large number of women in New England were left impoverished. This factor influenced literature by women, especially the "local colorists" of the last century who write about the traditional culture of the time. Keating discusses the fiction of Mary Wilkins Freeman (1852-1920) who offers a good example of this literary topic. Freeman captures the tragedy of older, single women who had to struggle under difficult circumstances.

8-46. Kehl, D. G. (1985). Thalia meets Tithonus: Gerontological wit and humor in literature. The Gerontologist, 25, 539-544.

Literature from the classical antiquity to the contemporary period is filled with examples of gerontological humor. Kehl identifies 9 distinct forms: (1) the foibles of aging; (2) what aging means; (3) the relativity of old age; (4) physical decline; (5) mental decline; (6) social relations; (7) youth and age; (8) black humor; and (9) breaking stereotypical views of old age. The author offers specific literary examples of humor in each category.

8-47. Kenyon, G. M. (1991). Homo viator: Metaphors of aging, authenticity, and meaning. In G. M. Kenyon, J. E. Birren, & J. J. F. Schroots (Eds.), Metaphors of aging in science and the humanities (pp. 17-35). New York: Springer Publishing Company.

The metaphor of homo viator refers to the human being as a traveler or pilgrim, and aging as a journey. Gerontologist employ this metaphor because of its flexibility. The journey of life may be long or short, easy or difficult, risky, ever-changing, hence, interesting. To be sure, this characterization of Kenyon's essay is too simplistic, but the metaphor he describes is indeed pervasive in gerontology.

8-48. Kerrigan, W. (1986). Life's iamb: The scansion of late creativity in the culture of the Renaissance. In K. Woodward, & M. M. Schwartz (Eds.), Memory and desire: Aging--literature--psychoanalysis (pp. 168-191). Bloomington, IN: Indiana University Press.

An exploration of the thesis that the creative recollection in tranquility of a momentous previous moment intensifies the experience is the subject of this essay. Shakespeare's The Tempest, Milton's Paradise Lost, and a physician Jean Baptiste Van Helmont provide examples of Kerrigan's central thesis.

8-49. Lefcowitz, B. F., & Lefcowitz, A. B. (1976). Old age in the modern literary imagination: An overview. Soundings, 59, 447-466.

In this survey of 19th and 20th century fictional works, the authors identify 4 basic patterns in the depiction of old age: (1) the older person as a model, e.g., Eudora Welty's "A Worn Path"; (2) the older person as a touchstone, e.g., Balzac's Père Goriot; (3) the older the person symbolizes societal oppression or spiritual death, e.g., Chekov's "Old Age"; and (4) the older person as a reflection of the absurdity of life, e.g., Muriel Spark's Memento Mori.

8-50. Lefcowitz, B., & Lefcowitz, A. (1984). Old age and the modern literary imagination. In L. Porter, L. M. Porter (eds.), Aging in literature (pp. 129-148). Troy, MI: International Book Publishers.

This essay is a slight modification of the previous entry (8-49).

8-51.   Leon, E. F. (1963).   Cicero on geriatrics.   The Gerontologist, 3(3, part I), 128-130.

Cicero's De Senectute limited his discussion of old age to upper middle-class males.   The main idea of this essay is to prepare for old age during youth.   The format of Cicero's work is a dialogue with Cato the elder as the central figure. Cato refutes several misconceptions about old age including: (1) the belief that old age reduces an individual's activity; (2) decline of memory; (3) physical decline; and (4) lack of pleasure.   Leon argues that many of the points made by Cicero anticipate modern scientific work in gerontology.

8-52.   Loughman, C. (1980a).   Eros and the elderly: A literary review.   The Gerontologist, 20, 182-187.

The fact that contemporary writers now write about the sexuality of older people in their fiction breaks down long held myths about older adults and their erotic needs.   Many sensitive accounts of eroticism in older adults show this as a physical desire and a psychological realization of a latent need.   Authors examined in this essay include John Barth, John Cheever, Saul Bellow, Eudora Welty, and V. S. Pritchett.

8-53.   Loughman, C. (1980b).   Literary views of the isolated elderly. Educational Gerontology, 5, 249-257.

Selected examples of contemporary literature show that physically and psychologically isolated older people are often portrayed in a hopeless and desperate situation.   A pervasive sense of diminution in the lives of older adults permeates much of 20th century literature, e.g., the poetry of Frost and Edward Arlington Robinson or the writings of Edward Albee, Lessing and Mannes.

8-54.   McKee, P. L. (Ed.) (1982).   Philosophical foundations of gerontology. New York: Human Sciences Press.

The 4 sections in this book contain reprinted excerpts from distinct parts: (1) classical philosophical readings; (2) ethical domains of aging; (3) epistemological aspects of aging; and (4) gerontology and the philosophy of science.   This anthology makes available in a single volume a number of significant philosophical treatises about aging.   A useful annotated bibliography is included. See 8-60.

8-55.   MacLam, H. (1985).   Critique of "Depictions of elderly Blacks in American literature."   Explorations in Ethnic Studies, 8(2), 30-31.

Several points in Deck's essay (see 8-28) are amplified: (1) the different depictions of older African-Americans by White and Black authors; and (2) the issue of reconciliation of the formal knowledge acquired by the young compared to the experiential wisdom of the older Black.

8-56. Mader, W. (1991). Aging and the metaphor of Narcissism. In G. M. Kenyon, J. E. Birren, & J. J. F. Schroots (Eds.), Metaphors of aging in science and the humanities (pp. 131-153). New York: Springer Publishing Company.

Equation of old age with narcissism is the central theme of this essay. According to Mader, the myth of narcissism, though primarily centered on youth, has implications for old age since the normal process of aging is antithetical to narcissism. Recognition of this fact has implications for psychotherapy with older adults. The author notes that in contemporary society the context of older people (unemployment, dependency, age-cohort voting power, etc.) facilitates narcissistic situations. It is often the case that older people fail to cope effectively with the implications of the prevailing narcissistic myth.

8-57. Magnan, R. (1984). Sex and senescence in medieval literature. In L. Porter, L. M. Porter (eds.), Aging in literature (pp. 13-30). Troy, MI: International Book Publishers.

In this selected overview of ageism and sexism in medieval literature, Magnan discusses the double standard of aging in which women lose their sexuality far sooner than men. Writers in the period do not view aging as a gradual process or a personal experience. The author notes that old age is distinct from youth in terms of biological, psychological, and moral characteristics.

8-58. Manning, G. F. (1989). Fiction and aging: "Ripeness is all." Canadian Journal on Aging, 8, 157-163.

The study of the humanities can play an essential role in understanding aging. Robert N. Butler's notion of the "life review" and Erik H. Erikson's "integrity" are complex themes that have been dealt with in a sensitive fashion in fictional accounts of the aging process. Writings by Muriel Spark, Tillie Olsen, Margaret Laurence, and Jessica Anderson illustrate this possibility.

8-59. Manning, G. F. (1991). Spinning the 'globe of memory': Metaphor, literature, and aging. In G. M. Kenyon, J. E. Birren, & J. J. F. Schroots (Eds.), Metaphors of aging in science and the humanities (pp. 37-55). New York: Springer Publishing Company.

Good literature admits and encourages multiple interpretations.   Common metaphors of aging include frailty and deterioration, age as a journey, and others. Manning alludes to literary works to support his statements. Metaphor, because of its subjective nature, is a particularly salient device for the stimulation of discussion of ideas on aging that may parallel nascent theories in other disciplines.

8-60.   Moody H. R. (1982).   Review of Philosophical foundations of gerontology ed. by P. L. McKee, New York: Human Sciences Press, 1982. The Gerontologist, 22, 341-342.

According to Moody, this volume fulfills a void in the area of humanistic gerontology. The publication of this book represents a positive step toward more interdisciplinary research on gerontological questions than in the past. This volume provides a compendium of many of the major issues that confront the field of gerontology today. See 8-54.

8-61. Moody, H. R. (1985). Review essay: Late life creativity & wisdom. The Gerontologist, 25, 95-98.

In this review of 2 books on creativity and old age (The crown of life by H. Munsterberg, San Diego, CA: Harcourt, Brace, Jovanovich, 1983, and Wisdom and age ed. by J-R. Staude, Berkeley, CA: Ross Books, 1981), Moody comments on 2 books which link creativity and wisdom with the final stage of life. The author of this review article also raises the issue of objectivity as related to social scientific and humanistic studies of gerontology.

8-62. Nakadate, N. (1985). Critique of "Depictions of elderly Blacks in American literature." Explorations in Ethnic Studies, 8(2), 28-29.

The author criticizes Deck's (see 8-28) essay for its brevity. A number of questions are raised which Nakadate hopes will be addressed by Deck and/or others in future research.

8-63. Nicholl, G. (1984-1985). The life review in five short stories about characters facing death. Omega, 15(1), 85-96.

5 short stories by well-known writers (Leo Tolstoy, Ernest Hemingway, Katherine Anne Porter, Will Cather, and Tillie Olsen) are analyzed to determine how their protagonists deal with death. Nicholl examines these stories in terms of 2 recent theories about death and dying, namely Elisabeth Kubler-Ross's fifth stage of the dying process (acceptance) and Robert N. Butler's life review and its consequences. A thorough examination of these works shows that current

notions and hypotheses about death are applicable to literature. For this reason, the author argues for the use of these materials in gerontology courses and programs.

8-64. Nuessel, F. (1985). Review of Aging in literature ed. by L. Porter, and L. M. Porter, Troy, MI: International Book Publishers, 1984 The Gerontologist, 25, 558-559.

In a favorable review of this anthology, it is noted that many negative depictions of old age and older adults appear in the various literatures represented. The volume represents an excellent critical introduction to the theme of aging in literature. See 8-4.

8-65. Parker, M. (1991). The great escape: The meaning of the great escape theme in the humanities and gerontology. Educational Gerontology, 17, 55-61.

The theme of the "great escape" refers to an older person who overcomes significant obstacles to reconcile the past and prepare for inevitable death. Parker subdivides this theme into 4 distinct elements: (1) the impulse; (2) the great escape; (3) the quest; and (4) the closure. The author alludes to several examples of this phenomenon in film and literature.

8-66. Philibert, M. (1974). The phenomenological approach to images of aging. Soundings, 57, 33-49.

In this essay, Philibert defines the term aging (the passing of time), but he points out that his real concern is the association of aging with other factors such as illness, growth, and decline. The author cites literary examples of old age since this is an excellent source of particular images of the phenomenon, most of which depict decline and social disgrace. Finally, some speculations about the science of gerontology and its future are offered.

8-67. Portales, M. (1989). Youth and age in American literature: The rhetoric of old men in the Mathers, Franklin, Adams, Cooper, Hawthorne, Melville, and James. New York: Peter Lang Publishing.

As its title states, this books treats the special figure of "the old man" in selected, well-known American writers. In all of these literary works, the old man serves as a character whose extended life experience provides knowledge and wisdom. Such personages theoretically have disadvantages, however, their value in a fictional work outweighs any difficulties. These protagonists offer the possibility to have reminiscences, stream-of-consciousness techniques and flashbacks.

8-68. Portnoy, E. J. (1990). The OBASUTE legend: caregiving insights in literature. Educational Gerontology, 16, 561-575.

Japan's folkloric legend of the OBASUTE, or the theme of abandonment and sacrifice of older adults, provides a pedagogical opportunity for fostering intercultural consciousness among university students. In this empirical study, a questionnaire was administered to 117 college students in Japan and the U. S. to determine their attitudes toward caregiving. Portnoy suggests that the use of Shichiro Fukasawa's short story about the legend in a class would provide a vehicle for the discussion of student attitudes toward caregiving of older adults.

8-69. Schroots, J. J. F. (1991). Metaphors of aging and complexity. In G. M. Kenyon, J. E. Birren, & J. J. F. Schroots (Eds.), Metaphors of aging in science and the humanities (pp. 219-243). New York: Springer Publishing Company.

This essay illustrates the use of metaphor in psychology. The metaphorical view of science holds that figurative language is used to create and develop theories. Gerontological metaphors such as metabolic clocks. Schroots notes that since variability is a major theme of aging, certain metaphors have been employed to convey this notion, namely, fuzzy sets, the hologram, and the fractal geometrical approach.

8-70. Schroots, J. J. F., Birren, J. E., & Kenyon, G. M. (1991). Metaphors and aging: An overview. In G. M. Kenyon, J. E. Birren, & J. J. F. Schroots (Eds.), Metaphors of aging in science and the humanities (pp. 1-16). New York: Springer Publishing Company.

In this overview, 3 major points are discussed: (1) theories of metaphor; (2) the role of metaphor in science and gerontology; and (3) the role of metaphor in intervention in the aging field. This essay provides an excellent introduction to the use, and function of metaphor in gerontology.

8-71. Seltzer, M. M. (1989). When fields collide or a view from gerontology. In T. M. Falkner & J. de Luce (Eds.), Old age in Greek and Latin literature (pp. 217-229). Albany, NY: State University of New York Press.

As a gerontologist, Seltzer is in a unique position to comment on the contacts of 2 quite different disciplines--gerontology and the humanities. One of the difficulties inherent in dealing with multi-disciplinary studies is an insufficient knowledge of the second area (gerontology or humanities). The author offers specific recommendations for the humanist who wishes to engage in the field of gerontology: (1) employ rigorous research techniques; (2) avoid stereotypes of older people; (3) recognize that old age has positive and negative aspects; (4) recognize that gerontology itself is an emerging field; and (5) be aware that multi-disciplinary work may be scorned.

8-72. Shephard, R. J. (1991). An exercise physiologist's perspective on metaphors of health and aging. In G. M. Kenyon, J. E. Birren, & J. J. F. Schroots (Eds.), Metaphors of aging in science and the humanities (pp. 185-198). New York: Springer Publishing Company.

Metaphors concerning health and aging are abundant. The "human machine" metaphor implies that the gerontologist will treat the patient as a machine subject, e.g., the "wear and tear" theory. Another prominent metaphor is the human computer whereby obsolescence is built into the system and "old computers" are discarded. A third metaphor is that of "human design" with the implication that the body is intended to wear out. Yet another common metaphor is aging as an increased probability of death, i.e., aging is a disease. Shephard ultimately argues for quantitative biology as a metaphor. This approach permits the description of aging as functional loss which is more comprehensible to people. Moreover, this metaphor facilitates procedures for slowing such loss.

8-73. Simmons, T. (1985). Critique of "Depictions of elderly Blacks in American literature." Explorations in Ethnic Studies, 8(2), 31-33.

In this note, Simmons takes issue with Deck's (see 8-28) assertion that the Uncle Remus is a racist stereotype. Rather, this critic asserts, Uncle Remus is a part of American popular culture.

8-74. Simonton, D. K. (1990). Creativity in the later years: Optimistic prospects for achievement. The Gerontologist, 30, 626-631.

In this essay, the author considers 7 factors that may influence creative productivity in later life: (1) the amount of the decrement; (2) negative effects of old age may be mitigated; (3) reduction in creative output does not necessarily reflect psychological impairment; (4) late life creativity corresponds to earlier creativity; (5) age decrement in creativity varies according to the discipline; (6) the quality-quantity ratio means that it is difficult to speak of a decrement on an item-by-item basis; and (7) late-life creative resurgence may take place.

8-75. Sohngen, M. (1975). The writer as an old woman. The Gerontologist, 15, 493-498.

The writings of 19 American and British women born prior to 1910 (e.g., Ayn Rand, Katherine Ann Porter, Jessamyn West) who continue to publish provide the sources of this essay. Each author's pertinent publications are described and discussed. Sohngen observes that the characteristics to be found in the women profiled are flexibility, a concern for the reader, and the ability to exert a great and sustained effort in their writing activities.

8-76. Somerville, R. M. (1972). The future of family relationships in middle and later years: Fiction. Family Coordinator, 21(4) 487-498.

In this review of selected fiction about middle-age and old age, Somerville discusses and defines current notions about these 2 life stages. Among the themes of old age are the following: remarriage, assistance networks, services, institutions, and communes. For each area, the author mentions specific, related fictional works.

8-77. Spector, S. I. (1973). Old age and the sages. International Journal of Aging and Human Development, 4, 199-209.

The Talmud contains many observations about old age. The definition of old age, the status of older people, positive and negative images, prescriptions for well being in old age, and the theme of death are all to be found in this collection of ancient Rabbinic writings which are the source of religious authority for Judaism.

8-78. Svoboda, C. P. (1977). Senescence in western philosophy. Educational Gerontology, 2, 219-235.

In a comprehensive review of the major philosophical writings from 4 distinct periods (ancient, medieval, modern, contemporary), Svoboda seeks to characterize senescence.   The author employed 4 principal themes: (1) descriptions and explanations of old age; (2) the psyche of the older person; (3) the power of older adults; and (4) the status or position of the older individual. In his concluding remarks, Svoboda notes that in all 4 periods studied, older adults are treated similarly in the philosophical treatises, i.e., as a period of loss, decline, and infirmity. Even though this picture is bleak, it is important to know the historical viewpoints on aging.

8-79. Walker, B. G. (1985). The crone: Woman of age, wisdom, and power. San Francisco: Harper & Row Publishers.

The "crone" is a symbolic old woman who populated the fringes of a male-dominated society. As a literary figure, the crone acknowledges no master, and is a powerful feminist symbol. This archetypal figure is traced in literature, history, and the arts. This monograph is a thorough study of the older female.

8-80. Weiland, S. (1990). Editorial. Gerontology and literary studies. The Gerontologist, 30, 435-436.

In his editorial, Weiland acknowledges the place of literature and the humanities in gerontological and geriatric studies. Nevertheless, a host of new, post-modern approaches to literary criticism has emerged in recent years. These evolving trends in the study of literature have implications for gerontological literary study. The author speculates that the recent theoretical developments (reader-response theory, the rhetoric of interpretation, deconstruction, etc.) in literature departments may find an application in gerontology.

8-81. Woodward, K. M. (1983). Instant repulsion: Decrepitude, the mirror stage, and the literary imagination. The Kenyon Review, 5, 43-66.

The human body as a symbol of the human condition is the point of departure for this essay. Old age has as its external manifestation certain common images such as wrinkles, and decrepitude. This symbolic representation has as one of its frequent manifestations the mirror image in literature. Woodward develops this metaphor in the rest of her essay.

8-82. Woodward, K. (1986). Reminiscence and the life review: Prospects and retrospects. In T. R. Cole, & S. A. Gadow (Eds.), What does it mean to grow old? Reflections from the humanities (pp. 135-161). Durham, NC: Duke University Press.

Literary characterizations are varied. One theme is that of dementia as depicted in Yashusi Inoue's novel Chronicle of my mother, and Marion Roach's essay on Alzheimer's disease in the New York Times Magazine. A second theme is that of the life review exemplified by Joyce Cary's To be a pilgrim, and Henry James' short story "The beast in the jungle." A final theme is the tape-recorded past as seen in Samuel Beckett's Krapp's last tape. All of these creative manifestations of themes related to old age demonstrate the need to confront oneself, as uncomfortable as this process may be.

8-83. Woodward, K. (1991). Aging and its discontents: Freud and other fictions. Bloomington, IN: Indiana University Press.

This volume contains a series of essays that deal with old age in the western literary, and psychoanalytical tradition. Among the works analyzed are Freud's essays, as well as works by Marcel Proust, Virginia Woolf, Eva Figes, Roland

Barthes, and Samuel Beckett. Woodward has taught courses on literature and aging and has published extensively on this subject. This critic's perspectives on aging are insightful and challenging and merit consultation.

8-84. Wyatt-Brown, A. M. (1989). The narrative/imperative: Fiction and the aging writer. Journal of Aging Studies, 3, 55-65.

Novel literary critical approaches combined with more traditional strategies provide the possibility of new insights into aging. Since gerontologists often raise questions of interest, and significance to literary scholars, a formalization of this type of scholarly relationship can yield revealing results. In this study, 2 older writers (E. M. Forster, and Virginia Woolf) are examined to demonstrate a procedure for combining literary theory and gerontological matters.

8-85. Yates, E. F. (1991). Aging as prolonged morphogenesis: A topobiologic sorcerer's apprentice. In G. M. Kenyon, J. E. Birren, & J. J. F. Schroots (Eds.), Metaphors of aging in science and the humanities (pp. 199-218). New York: Springer Publishing Company

The use of metaphor in biology provides a means of explaining certain elements of the complex nature of this process. Yates provides a detailed account of the use of figurative speech in the biological sciences.

NATIONAL AND ETHNIC LITERATURES

8-86. Allen, R. (1989). Old age in Arabic literature. In P. v. D. Bagnell & P. S. Soper (Eds.), Perceptions of aging in literature: A cross-cultural study (pp. 113-130). New York: Greenwood Press.

Arabic literature is heterogenous, thus reflective of the diversity of the distinct Arabic-speaking nations of the Middle East. Selections from 7 poets and 1 short story writer (Najib Mahfuz, 1911, Nobel Prize for literature, 1988) are included in this essay.

8-87. Archambault, P. J. (1989). From centrality to expendability: The aged in French literature. In P. v. D. Bagnell & P. S. Soper (Eds.), Perceptions of aging in literature: A cross-cultural study (pp. 51-69). New York: Greenwood Press.

French literature offers a rich array of selections about older adults and aging. Accounts of older people include the medieval French epic as well as works by

André Gide (1869-1951, Nobel prize for literature, 1947). Archambault notes that in the nineteenth century, the depiction of older characters shifted from veneration to exploitation which mirrors the rise of the industrialization and the consequential changes effected by that social transformation. In the late twentieth century, a literary indifference to old age has become evident despite demographic evidence of an expanded group of older citizens. Among the literary passages included are poetry by Ronsard, Victor Hugo, Alfred de Vigny, and prose by Montaigne, Balzac, Flaubert, and Zola.

8-88. Fallis, R. C. (1989). "Grow old along with me": Images of older people in British and American literature. In P. v. D. Bagnell & P. S. Soper (Eds.), Perceptions of aging in literature: A cross-cultural study (pp. 35-50). New York: Greenwood Press.

The literature of aging from Great Britain and the United States treats a variety of themes including intergenerational contact and conflict, engagement and disengagement, and insightful reminiscence. Often older people are perceived as either a threat or a burden in much of this literature. In more recent literature, old age has come to the forefront in many instances. The older character is no longer anomalous or peripheral. Literary selections from Shakespeare, Tennyson, Robert Browning, Mathew Arnold, Robert Frost, and May Sarton are included.

8-89. Gunn, E. (1989). The honored aged in Chinese literature. In P. v. D. Bagnell & P. S. Soper (Eds.), Perceptions of aging in literature: A cross-cultural study (pp. 145-165). New York: Greenwood Press.

The tradition of old age in Chinese literature is quite extensive. The literary examples that deal with old age include proverbs, personal testimony, poetry, and short stories. Respect for older people is a Chinese cultural tradition. Nevertheless, the profound political changes of the twentieth century have caused a negative reaction against the earlier Confucian customs. Selections from Confucius (fifth century B.C.), Mencius (third century B.C.), Lin Yutang (1895-1976), Meng Chiao (751-814), and Li Fei-kan (1904-) are among the writers included.

8-90. Lichtblau, M. R. (1989). Aging as cultural reflection in Hispanic American literature. In P. v. D. Bagnell & P. S. Soper (Eds.), Perceptions of aging in literature: A cross-cultural study (pp. 99-111). New York: Greenwood Press.

Although there is no clearly discernible tradition of a literature of aging in the Hispanic American creative writing, noteworthy examples, in fact, exist.

Selections from Alonso de Ercilla (1533-1594), René Marqués (1919-1981), Florencio Sánchez (1875-1910), José Donoso (1924-), and Gabriel García Márquez (1928, Nobel Prize for literature, 1982), and Carlos Fuentes (1928-)

8-91. Roberts, L. (1989). Portrayal of the elderly in classical Greek and Roman literature. In P. v. D. Bagnell & P. S. Soper (Eds.), Perceptions of aging in literature: A cross-cultural study (pp. 17-33). New York: Greenwood Press.

Greek literature offers variation in attitudes toward old age and older people. Depictions include both negative (infirmity, poverty) and positive (wisdom, experience) aspects. Just as its Greek counterpart, the Roman literature of aging is sporadic and incomplete. Once again, the image of old age and old people is diverse.   Greek literary selections include Sophocles (496-406 B.C.), Aristophanes (45-385 B.C.), Euripides (485-406 B.C.), and Plato (429-327 B.C.).   Roman literary examples feature Horace (655-8 B.C.), Seneca (4 B.C-65 A.D.), and Cicero (106-43 B.C.).

8-92. Schneider, G. K. (1989). Aging in German and Austrian Literature. In P. v. D. Bagnell & P. S. Soper (Eds.), Perceptions of aging in literature: A cross-cultural study (pp. 71-86). New York: Greenwood Press.

The theme of old age is represented in a number of literary works in Germany, Austria, and Switzerland. Selections from writers who have written in German are Goethe (1749-1832), Schopenhauer (1788-1860), Stifter (1805-1868), Schnitzler (1862-1931), Hesse (1877-1962, Nobel Prize for literature 1946), and Brecht (1898-1956).

8-93. Skord, V. (1989). "Withered Blossoms": Aging in Japanese literature. In P. v. D. Bagnell & P. S. Soper (Eds.), Perceptions of aging in literature: A cross-cultural study (pp. 131-143). New York: Greenwood Press.

Although Western readers take for granted that the Japanese have a deep-seated respect for older people, the topic of old age in literature reflects ambivalence and deeply felt emotion. Old age is seen as a period of decay and renewal. Japan's literature reflects this dichotomous viewpoint. The selections included in this essay demonstrate this, e.g., Ryokan (1758-1831), Kawabata Yasunari (1899-1972), and Mishima Yukio (1925-1970).

8-94. Stacy, R. H. (1989). "No Joy": Old age in Russian literature. In P. v. D. Bagnell & P. S. Soper (Eds.), Perceptions of aging in literature: A cross-cultural study (pp. 87-97). New York: Greenwood Press.

Old age in Russian literature features older men as idealized personifications while older women tend to be represented in a negative fashion. Literary selections include passages from Turgenev (1818-1883), Mikhail Sholokov (1905-1984, Nobel Prize in literature, 1965), and Alexander Kushner (1936-).

AUTOBIOGRAPHIES AND DIARIES

8-95. Berman, H. J. (1986). To flame with a wildlife: Florida Scott-Maxwell's experience of old age. The Gerontologist, 26, 321-324.

Personal journals constitute a type of case study for a source of information on the significance of aging. Scott-Maxwell's The measure of my days is a source of information on the old-old, late life individuation, and an exemplar of successful aging. Intimate journals serve as an important additional perspective which complements traditional methodologies.

8-96. Cole, T. R., & Premo, T. (1986-1987). The pilgrimage of Joel Andrews: Aging in the autobiography of a Yankee farmer. International Journal of Aging and Human Development, 24, 79-85.

Joel Andrews (1777-1865), a New England farmer, wrote an autobiography published in 1850. From this personal account, Cole and Premo examine Andrews' reactions to death and aging within the context of his own historical framework. The authors of this study indicate differences in the notions of health and vitality in old age that are distinct from those of contemporary society. More important, however, is the autobiographical chronicling of Andrews' increasing focus on the spiritual domain of his life with the passage of time.

8-97. Donow, H. S. (1991). Am I my father's keeper? Sons as caregivers. The Gerontologist, 31, 709-711.

In this review of 2 non-fiction books that treat the theme of sons who care for their terminally ill fathers: (1) Mirrored lives by Tom Koch (Praeger: New York, 1990); and (2) Patrimony by Phillip Roth (New York: Simon and Schuster, 1991). Both works deal with an intensely emotional time for these writers. Donow believes, however, that Roth's book is better stylistically than is Koch's. A sub-genre of literature descriptive of the care of an older parent by a child is likely to increase given the demographics of this society.

8-98. Hill-Lubin, M. A. (1991). The African-American grandmother in autobiographical works by Frederick Douglas, Langston Hughes, and Maya

Angelou. International Journal of Aging and Human Development, 33, 173-185.

Autobiographies provide important information on the role of the African-American grandmother. This person has 3 important and distinct functions within her culture: (1) a person is full of activity, involvement, hope, and dignity; (2) an individual who maintains and distributes the family history, wisdom, and black culture; and (3) the person who preserves and transmits values that support the family, and the community. Such a role model can be used for future generations.

8-99. Kebric, R. (1983). Aging in Pliny's Letters: A view from the second century A. D. The Gerontologist, 23, 538-545.

The correspondence of Pliny the Younger (61-113 AD) provides the reader with a first-hand account of how old age was perceived at the time of the Roman empire. Several key passages provide insights into intergenerational contacts, retirement, attitudes about aging, and the problems of older people.

8-100. Porter, L. M. (1984). Montaigne's final revisions: An Eriksonian assessment. In L. Porter, L. M. Porter (eds.), Aging in literature (pp. 49-58). Troy, MI: International Book Publishers.

In a review of three versions of Montaigne's essays (A-version = 1571-1580, B-version = 1580-1588, and C-version = 1588-1592), Porter seeks to determine the French philosopher's capacity for creative and original thinking in the latter stages of his life within the framework of Erik Erikson's division of life into 8 separate stages. The comparison of the added materials in Montaigne's writings permits Porter to assess how the great French writer faces death and achieves maturity emotionally and practically.

8-101. West, P. (1989). Holographic memory in Nabokov and Nestor. Journal of Aging Studies, 3, 163-173.

In a discussion of memory in the Vladimir Nabokov's autobiography, as well as in the figure of Nestor in Ovid's metamorphoses, West decries the 2-dimensional, scientific approach to the study of memory. There is much to be learned in studying the associative memory found in creative writers in the oral or written tradition. Such accounts reveal the creative element of human memory.

8-102. Wyatt-Brown, A. M. (1989b). Walker Percy: Autobiographical fiction and the aging process. Journal of Aging Studies, 3, 81-89.

The author raises the issue of why Walker Percy's writings should be of interest to gerontologists since he wrote very little about aging in his works. The answer lies, precisely, in its avoidance. Wyatt-Brown speculates that, once Percy's earlier traumas were overcome, a reduction in creative rigor and an acceptance of life's limitations have appeared in this Southern writer's literary efforts.

DRAMA

8-103. Asp, C. (1986). "The clamor of Eros": Freud, aging, and King Lear. In K. Woodward, & M. M. Schwartz (Eds.), Memory and desire: Aging-- literature--psychoanalysis (pp. 192-204). Bloomington, IN: Indiana University Press.

A Freudian explanation of Shakespeare's tragic Lear figure is offered in this essay. Lear seeks refuge as an infant to be cared for by his own children, yet he is denied this desire. The tragedy in this play, according to Asp, lies in the king's inability to learn anything from his situation despite the enormous suffering of all involved.

8-104. Banziger, G. (1979). Intergenerational communication in prominent Western drama. The Gerontologist, 19, 471-480.

The dichotomous theme of virtuous youth and malevolent old age occurs frequently in western dramatic pieces. A discussion of writings by many of the best known playwrights is included: (1) Aeschylus and Sophocles; (2) Plautus and Terence; (3) Shakespeare; (4) Molière; (5) George Bernard Shaw; (6) Eugene O'Neill and Arthur Miller. Intergenerational contact (living arrangements, attitudes and preferences of older people relative to contact with their children, and the types of intergenerational encounters) is discussed. Subsequently, a comparison of the factual situation with that depicted in the dramas under discussion ensues.

8-105. Berman, L., & Nelson, J. (1986-1987). Voltaire's portrayal of old age. International Journal of Aging and Human Development, 24, 161-169.

In this scrutiny of 50 plays written by Voltaire over a 65-year period. The authors of this essay have reached several conclusions: (1) older males predominate; (2) older women are depicted less favorably than older males which reflects either literary convention or bias; (3) older characters appear throughout Voltaire's writing career with a consistency of characterization; (4)

the specific traits of Voltaire's characters derive from their personalities and not their age; and (5) wisdom is the one characteristic ascribed to old age.

8-106. Bronsen, D. (1978). Consuming struggle versus killing time: Preludes to dying in the dramas of Ibsen and Beckett. In S. F. Spicker, K. M. Woodward, & D. Van Tassel (Eds.), Aging and the elderly: Humanistic perspectives on gerontology (pp. 261-281). Atlantic Highlands, NJ: Humanities Press, Inc.

Noting that the apparent differences between the realistic drama of the great nineteenth century Norwegian dramatist and the grotesque dramaturgy of twentieth century Irish playwright Beckett are significant, Bronsen compares the protagonist's approach to impending death in works by both authors. The author concludes that Ibsen's characters are driven while those of Beckett are alienated. Nevertheless, in the creative works of both authors, the central characters experience a sense of despair and defeat.

8-107. Cox, E. H. (1943). Shakespeare and some conventions of old age. Studies in Philology, 39, 36-46.

Shakespeare's works contained conventionalized images of old age. Perusal of the English dramatist's works reveals a number of commonplaces. Cox points out that a number of Shakespeare's references to old age are actually conventional even though they have not been so recognized. Evidence presented in this study shows that Shakespeare employed many existing literary formulae to describe old age.

8-108. Daalder, J. (1986). The role of "senex" in Kyd's The Spanish Tragedy. Comparative Drama, 20, 247-260.

The function of the "old man" in Thomas Kyd's well known play shows that the senex functions as a spokesperson for ideas found in the works of the Roman tragedian Seneca.

8-109. Datan, N. (1988). The Oedipus cycle: Developmental mythology, Greek tragedy, and the sociology of knowledge. International Journal of Aging and Human Development, 27, 1-10.

The author argues that Freud's Oedipus complex is a metaphorical borrowing to describe a particular psychological situation. In contrast, a careful reading of the second play in Sophocles' Oedipus cycle, Oedipus at Colonus, shows that this work represents the consciousness of the developmental stages in the life cycle as well as intergenerational dependence and the inevitability of generational succession.

8-110. Dowling, J. (1983). Moratín's creation of the comic role for the older actress. Theatre Survey, 24, 55-63.

Dowling shows that the Spanish dramatist Leandro Fernández de Moratín (1760-1828) was a significant innovator in the Spanish theatre by creating a comic role for the older actress. This innovation subsequently paved the way for future comic and serious roles for older women in the theatre of Spain.

8-111. Draper, J. W. (1940). The old age of King Lear. Journal of English and Germanic Philology, 39, 527-540.

In this essay, Draper discusses and documents in detail several basic elements of old age in Shakespeare's King Lear. Topics examined include: (1) the actual age of King Lear; (2) Elizabethan notions of developmental stages in life; (3) the actual stages of King Lear and his reaction to these periods.

8-112. Draper, J. W. (1946). Shakespeare's attitude toward old age. Journal of Gerontology, 1, 48-51.

In a brief overview of Shakespeare's attitudes toward old age as revealed in his writings, Draper notes the physical side focused on defects and infirmity. The psychological domain of aging, demonstrated in his later works, shows a more sympathetic attitude toward this stage of life as seen in King Lear.

8-113. Falkner, T. M. (1989). The wrath of Alcemene: Gender, authority and old age in Euripides' Children of Heracles. In T. M. Falkner & J. de Luce (Eds.), Old age in Greek and Latin literature (pp. 114-131). Albany, NY: State University of New York Press.

In literary tradition, the stereotype of the vengeful woman forms an important part of this dramatic work. Euripides' play makes this cultural artifact in which an older woman acquires power and independence and employs this newfound influence for evil ends. Falkner speculates about the extent that this literary depiction of the aggressive and domineering older woman reflects Athenian times. Some evidence about the culture of that time suggests that the stereotype derived from certain elements of the social systems that cast women in that real-life role.

8-114. Herrero, J. (1984). Celestina: The aging prostitute as witch. In L. Porter, L. M. Porter (eds.), <u>Aging in literature</u> (pp. 31-47). Troy, MI: International Book Publishers.

The personality of the Celestina, an older woman, prostitute, and witch, is powerful, magnetic, and cunning, and sly. In this Spanish masterpiece, Celestina is clearly aware of her old age and its effect on her. Because the main character of this play/novel no longer possesses her youthful charms, she must rely on her skill at manipulating others who possess this trait to achieve her goals and desires. Ultimately, Celestina destroys herself by breaking all of her society's moral rules.

8-115. Hubbard, T. K. (1989). Old men in the youthful plays of Aristophanes. In T. M. Falkner & J. de Luce (Eds.), <u>Old age in Greek and Latin literature</u> (pp. 90-113). Albany, NY: State University of New York Press.

In a reinterpretation of the function of older characters and the chorus in Aristophanes' dramatic works, Hubbard argues that older persons serve as spokespersons of the audience in a period when traditional values are undermined by new political leadership. Hubbard views old age in the exant work of this Greek playwright as a symbol of rejuvenation in the Athenian spirit. Furthermore, it is possible that the evolution of the old men in Aristophanes dramatic works reflects the author's own artistic development.

8-116. Kearns, T. B. (1978). Prisoner to palsy: A study of old age in Shakespeare's history plays (Doctoral dissertation, Indiana University at Bloomington, 1978). <u>Dissertation Abstracts International</u>, <u>39</u>, 6777A.

A preliminary discussion provides an overview and introduction to classical, medieval, and renaissance works on old age. The remainder of this study analyzes in chronological order those plays of Shakespeare that deal with older characters in order to determine any changes in their depiction. Kearns observes that there is an increasing reliance on older characters as a source of drama. Moreover, Shakespeare became more sympathetic to old age, and its problems.

8-117. Mignon, E. (1947). <u>Crabbed age and youth: The old men and women in restoration comedy of manners</u>. Durham, NC: Duke University Press.

Old age in this study deals with the literary conventions established for its depiction in the comedy of manners (1660-1700) and not Restoration comedy in general.   6 chapters are devoted to specific authors: (1) Etherege, (2) Wycherley, (3) Dryden, Shadwell and Aphra Behn, (4) Congreve,

(5) Vanbrugh, and (6) Farquhar. Mignon views the depiction of old age as a metaphor for a rejection of the values of the previous generation.

8-118. Miles, L. W. (1940). Shakespeare's old men. English Literary History, 7, 286-299.

Identifiably older male characters in Shakespeare's writings are relatively scarce. In many instances, it is difficult to determine the age of a particular person (e.g., Shylock). Nevertheless, when they do appear, the older men possess a number of distinctive characteristics, e. g., irritability (King Lear), and foolishness (Polonius). Many of Miles' examples of old men in Shakespeare's plays are negative.

8-119. Porter, L. (1984). King Lear and the crisis of retirement. In L. Porter, L. M. Porter (eds.), Aging in literature (pp. 59-71). Troy, MI: International Book Publishers.

In this interpretation of Shakespeare's King Lear, Porter argues that the intergenerational problems experienced by the King result from his personality and not from senescence. Lear's final wisdom thus comes not from his age but rather from his ability to make sense of his life and his actions after his period of madness. According to Porter, the real tragedy of the play derives from the King's failure to engage in a meaningful life review in order to take account of the meaning of his life.

8-120. Ricciardelli, R. M. (1973). King Lear and the theory of disengagement. The Gerontologist, 13, 148-157.

The theory of disengagement is the approach employed in this analysis of Shakespeare's classic drama. In her application of this theory to Lear's plight, Ricciardelli also discusses more recent research on the disengagement theory of old age. This study is a good example of how an interdisciplinary approach to the study of aging may foster discussion along humanistic lines.

8-121. Schwab, G. (1986). The intermediate area between life and death: On Samuel Beckett's The Unnamable. In K. Woodward, & M. M. Schwartz (Eds.), Memory and desire: Aging--literature--psychoanalysis (pp. 205-217). Bloomington, IN: Indiana University Press.

Many of Beckett's characters are old or dying men who ruminate on their infirmity and degeneration. Schwab elects to read the Irish playwright's The Unnamable as the speech of an old man dealing with impending death. In doing so, the author believes that Beckett provides a non-stereotypic view of old age which presents this stage of life as a unique experience.

8-122. Smith, H. (1976). Bare ruined choirs: Shakespearean variations on the theme of old age. Huntington Library Quarterly, 39, 233-249.

William Shakespeare's views of old age are the subject of this essay which also provides the reader with a picture of the period and locale of the famed English writer.   Carefully selected citations from Shakespeare's sonnets and plays provide the sources of this focused analysis of that author's views on old age which include pathos, sympathy and formulaic farce.

8-123. Thomas, L. S. (1977). Krapp: Beckett's aged Narcissus. CEA Critic, 39, 9-11.

Samuel Beckett's brief play Krapp's Last Tape features a solitary character who functions as an aged Narcissus. Thomas insightfully demonstrates how the tape recordings made at earlier stages of the protagonist's life, and played again in later life, constitute an aural compulsion akin to Narcissus's visual obsession with himself.

8-124. Van Nortwick, T. (1989). "Do Not Go Gently . . ." Oedipus at Colonus and the psychology of aging. In T. M. Falkner & J. de Luce (Eds.), Old age in Greek and Latin literature (pp. 132-156). Albany, NY: State University of New York Press.

Noting that the psychology of aging is a relatively recent area of study, Van Nortwick seeks to apply recent advances in cross-cultural patterns of aging to Oedipus at Colonus. This approach to critical analysis of a classic Greek play is novel. The loss of physical strength and its substitution by an enhanced, albeit passive role in society is one of the ways in which the hero of this work retains self-esteem and personal prestige. This acquisition of a new type of power is seen to be a healthy response to the way in which older adults face their impending death.

NOVELS

8-125. Back, K. W. (1978). Old people in contemporary novels: A study of style and content. Educational Gerontology, 3, 165-173.

The author selected 160 novels published in the U.S. from 1931-1970 as the data base for this study. From each work, 5 samples of 3 pages each were examined to determine such factors as setting, and age and sex of characters. The results of the study show that except for the period of WW-II, the number of older characters has been steadily increasing during the 40-year period under review. Back notes that subject matter of a novel plays a role in the inclusion of older characters. Furthermore, the author notes that the more simple a novel is the more likely there will be older protagonists.

8-126. Berdes, C. (1981). Winter tales: Fiction about aging. The Gerontologist, 21, 121-125.

An overview of 30 recent fictional accounts of aging and older adults is the subject of this review essay. Berdes provides capsulized summaries of the works reviewed. Among the important works are those of 2 Noble prize-winners: Saul Bellow's Mr. Sammler's Planet, and Isaac Beshevis Singer's Old Love. Other writers include: Elizabeth Taylor's Mrs. Palfrey at the Claremont, May Sarton's As we are now, and Paul Theroux's Picture Palace. The author notes that fiction in which the themes of aging and older adults are prominent provide us with excellent instantiations of a process.

8-127. Charles, D. C., & Charles, L. A. (1979-1980). Charles Dicken's old people. International Journal of Aging and Human Development, 10, 231-2337.

A total of 121 characters were identified in this analysis of selected works (novels, short stories, Boz sketches) of Charles Dickens. Characters over 50 were identified as old. Their level of involvement was ascertained (protagonist, essential, somewhat involved, and minor role). Next, the personality characteristics (realistic, sympathetic, bland, absurd, negative, villainous) of each character was determined. The following general conclusions emerge: (1) older males outnumber older females by a 2:1 margin; (2) only 2 older characters are protagonists; (3) over 50% of the characters are sympathetic and 25% are negative. In summary, Dickens' older characters manifest a diversity which is not stereotypical, although older females are underdeveloped.

8-128. Donow, H. S. (1990) Two approaches to the care of the elder parent: A study of Robert Anderson's I Never Sang for My Father and Sawako Ariyoshi's Kokotsu no hito [The Twilight Years]. The Gerontologist, 30, 486-490.

A comparative literary approach provides a cross-cultural account of an American (R. S. Anderson) and a Japanese (S. Ariyoshi) response to the care of an older parent. In the former, the children are unwilling and unable to care for the father, while in the latter, the children accept great hardship to care for the paternal parent. Both works raise ethical questions about care of aging parents.

8-129. Festa-McCormick, D. (1984). Proustian old age, or the key to time recaptured. In L. Porter, L. M. Porter (Eds.), Aging in literature (pp. 105-113). Troy, MI: International Book Publishers.

A particular section of Proust's Remembrance of Things Past, the reception at Guermantes, provides Festa-McCormick with the opportunity to speculate about old age in the French author's famed novel. The protagonist's perceptions of the older people at the reception symbolizes Proust's view of this stage of life as a pathway to death or the opportunity for rebirth.

8-130. Gray, E. F. (1984). Balzac's myth of rejuvenation. In L. Porter, L. M. Porter (Eds.), Aging in literature (pp. 73-83). Troy, MI: International Book Publishers.

In his discussion of Balzac's conception of old age, Gray notes that the French writer's most important work on the topic of aging and death is La peau de chagrin. In this tale, Balzac's protagonist faces the dilemma of living a long and secure life or a brief and exuberant one. The author of this essay argues that many of Balzac's later works feature this dichotomy.

8-131. Knapp, B. L. (1984). Life/death: A journey (Yasunari Kawabata). In L. Porter, L. M. Porter (Eds.), Aging in literature (pp. 115-128). Troy, MI: International Book Publishers.

2 Japanese novels The Master of Go, and The Sound of the Mountain by Yasunari Kawabat are examined critically in an effort to understand the Asian sense of death and dying. Aging and dying are seen to be normal transitions and ought not to be feared. This essay provides interesting observations about the non-Western viewpoints on these issues.

8-132. Loughman, C. (1977). Novels of senescence: A new naturalism. The Gerontologist, 17, 79-84.

In this essay, 4 novels that address old age and aging are discussed: (1) Momento Mori (Muriel Spark, 1958); (2) Diary of a Mad Old Man (Junichiro Tanzaki, 1965); (3) Mr. Sammler's Planet (Saul Bellow, 1970); and (4) Ending Up (Kingsley Amis, 1974). Loughman examines the content of each novel and concludes that each one presents a rather grim picture of the final stages of life.

8-133. Magnan, R. J. (1985). Aspects of senescence in the work of Eustache Deschamps (Doctoral dissertation, Indiana University, 1985). <u>Dissertation Abstracts International</u>, <u>46</u>, 1621A.

The observations on old age by this fourteenth century French writer have received little previous attention. Deschamps' depiction of senescence is one of the most comprehensive to be found in medieval literature and hence constitutes a valuable reference work. Though traditional in its depiction of old age, care must be exercised to consider these poems as autobiographical or simple sociological reflections of the period in which they were written. The original copy of this dissertation at Indiana University at Bloomington has been declared lost.

8-134. Moss, W. G. (1978). Why the anxious fear?: Aging and death in the works of Turgenev. In S. F. Spicker, K. M. Woodward, & D. Van Tassel (eds.), <u>Aging and the elderly: Humanistic perspective in gerontology</u> (pp. 241-260). Atlantic Highlands, NJ: Humanistic Press.

Analysis of the great Russian writer Turgenev reveals an overall fear and loathing of death even though its inevitability managed to end many a protagonist's suffering. Youth, on the other hand, is contrasted with old age in a positive way. Moss speculates on why Turgenev feared death. In particular, Moss wonders if the Russian novelist suffered from a neurosis about death since he is unable to view old age as an opportune time to achieve important inner growth and positive personal development.

8-135. Porter, L. M. (1984). Farce and idealization: Dostoevsky's ambivalence toward aging. In L. Porter, L. M. Porter (Eds.), <u>Aging in literature</u> (pp. 85-113). Troy MI: International Book Publishers.

According to Porter, the aging process was a preoccupation of Dostoevsky. The focus of this essay is the sexuality of the older characters in the famed Russian author's fiction. The author concludes that throughout Dostoevsky writings, an ambivalent attitude toward sexuality in his older characters persists by demonstrating that older protagonists cannot be both wise and nurturant while also being sexual.

8-136. Ragland-Sullivan, E. (1986). The phenomenon of aging in Oscar Wilde's <u>Picture of Dorian Gray</u>: A Lacanian view. In K. Woodward, & M. M. Schwartz (Eds.), <u>Memory and desire: Aging--literature--psychoanalysis</u> (pp. 114-133). Bloomington, IN: Indiana University Press.

Psychological analyses of Wilde's well-known novel are numerous.   In her essay, Ragland-Sullivan applies Lacan's notions about the human life cycle to an understanding of this creative work.   The morbid fear of aging portrayed in Wilde's only novel is subjected to critical, literary, and psychoanalytical scrutiny in this revealing essay.

8-137.   Sohngen, M. (1977).   The experience of old age as depicted in contemporary novels.   The Gerontologist, 17, 70-78.

A survey of The Book Review Digest for the years 1950-1973 and novels reviewed in the Sunday New York Times Book Review form the data base for this study.   Themes found in these works of fiction include institutionalization of the old, retirement, isolation, segregated living, and intergenerational conflict. Many of the plots contain elements of Robert N. Butler's theory of the life review.   Sohngen suggests 3 courses in which the novels enumerated in an extensive annotated bibliography (pp. 72-78) may be used: (1) undergraduate programs of gerontology; (2) continuing education courses such as "The Philosophy of Aging"; and (3) a continuing education course on the contemporary novel.

8-138.   Sohngen, M. (1981).   Update: The experience of old age as depicted in contemporary novels: A supplementary bibliography.   The Gerontologist, 21, 203.

The author adds 5 more annotated entries to complement the one contained in her original essay (see 8-137).

8-139.   Sohngen, M. (1987).   The contemporary senex: A review essay.   The Gerontologist, 27, 538-539.

The senex or old man derives from the Greco-Latin literary tradition.   This stereotypic figure functioned as a primary laughable character and a source of much derisive humor.   According to Sohngehn, 3 recent novels, (The last good time by R. Bausch, A loving place by M. Dintenfass, and In the dark by R. M. Lamming) all feature an old protagonist who evokes an empathetic response in the reader.   Each of these novels presents an older male personage in a sensitive and non-stereotypic fashion.

8-140.   Sokoloff, J. M. (1986).   Character and aging in Moll Flanders.   The Gerontologist, 26, 681-686.

The eighteenth century novel Moll Flanders contains notions on aging and the life cycle that presage twentieth-century notions on this subject.   The life of

Defoe's female protagonist is presented from the perspective of a person who is 70.   Distinct stages in Moll Flanders' life are described corresponding to contemporary notions of stages in a life cycle.   The roughly decennial descriptions of the protagonist's exploits reveal Flanders' success in dealing effectively with the particular problems and adversities encountered in each stage of life.

8-141. Sokoloff, J. M. (1987). The margin that remains: A study of aging in literature. New York: Peter Lang.

6 novels (published 1722 to 1925) form the data base for this study of the evolution of the representation of human aging.   Sokoloff's investigation seeks to relate the writer's view of aging to the period in which the author wrote.   The novels studied are: Moll Flanders (Daniel Defoe), Persuasion (Jane Austen), Jane Eyre (Charlotte Bronte), Middlemarch (George Eliot), The Ambassadors (Henry James), and Mrs. Dalloway (Virginia Woolf).

8-142. Wolf, M. A. (1987). Human Development, gerontology, and self-development through the writings of May Sarton. Educational Gerontology, 13, 289-295.

In this essay, Wyatt-Brown describes an innovative technique for teaching a course in human development.   The method employed includes the writing of a journal to record personal reactions to the reading of 3 novels by May Sarton. Through this process, students become aware of the problems faced by older adults. The author argues that such an effective learning process should be an essential component in the education of students who aspire to work with older adults.

8-143. Woodward, K. (1986). The mirror stage of old age. In K. Woodward, & M. M. Schwartz (Eds.), Memory and desire: Aging--literature--psychoanalysis (pp. 97-113). Bloomington, IN: Indiana University Press.

In her careful examination of Marcel, the protagonist in The past recaptured, Woodward psychoanalyzes this character through a triadic application of hypotheses of old age found in the works of Freud, Lacan, and de Beauvoir. In particular, Woodward speculates about a development stage (the mirror stage) in later life when the individual confronts the biological reality of aging with repudiation and repulsion. This internal struggle against an irresistible element of life may cause people to fight the external manifestations of death with intensity.

8-144. Wyatt-Brown, A. M. (1984). From fantasy to pathology: Images of aging in the novels of Barbara Pym. Human Values and Aging Newsletter, 6, 5-8.

The British novelist, Barbara Pym (1913-1980), wrote several novels about unmarried, aging women. In her earlier works, these protagonists are depicted as positive, happy, well-adjusted people. One of her novels, Quartet in Autumn, deals with four aging characters who face the problems and difficulties of aging. The death of one of the protagonists ultimately liberates the remaining 3.

8-145. Wyatt-Brown, A. M. (1986). The loathly lady and the Edwardian statue: Life in pensioner hotels. The Gerontologist, 26, 207-210.

Keith Colquhoun's Kiss of life, and Elizabeth Taylor's Mrs. Palfrey at the Claremont are 2 contemporary novels that address the situation of older women pensioners. The protagonist in each work is memorable and each character faces the problems of old age and death differently, albeit with dignity. In both novels, the older women are unique and provide insights into how a person may surmount the not insignificant difficulties of loss and decline in later life with dignity.

8-146. Wyatt-Brown, A. M. (1988). Late style in the novels of Barbara Pym and Penelope Mortimer. The Gerontologist, 28, 835-839.

The work of 2 British novelists is the subject of this essay on "late style" in creative artists. This issue relates to the question of whether late style reflects continuity or change. Because Pym and Mortimer provide samples of creative writing over a lifetime, a comparison and contrast of their early and late writing styles is possible. Both writers demonstrate a mixture of continuity and change in their style. Moreover, each writer shows an increased creativity in later years.

POETRY

8-147. Bertman, S. (1989). The ashes and the flame: Passion and aging in classical poetry. In T. M. Falkner & J. de Luce (Eds.), Old age in Greek and Latin literature (pp. 157-171). Albany, NY: State University of New York Press.

A panoramic view of old age in Greek and Latin poetry from Homer to Ausonius reveals a correlation of old age with loss of sexual desirability, especially in the case of older women. Bertman also addresses the issue of sexuality in older adults depicted in this literary source. In general, however, the feelings of women are absent in the extant poems that treat love and desire in old age.

8-148.   Clark, M. (1980).   The poetry of aging: Views of old age in contemporary American poetry. The Gerontologist, 20, 186-191.

The data base for this study derives from 120 poems written by 22 contemporary American poets over 60. Clark sought to determine the themes and concerns of older poets about old age. Among the recurrent themes are the following: (1) vigor in old age; (2) general perspectives on old age and older adults; (3) old age as a period of wisdom and reflection; and (4) love relationships.

8-149.   Clay, J. S. (1989).   The old man in the garden: Georgic 4.116-148. In T. M. Falkner & J. de Luce (Eds.), Old age in Greek and Latin literature (pp. 183-194). Albany, NY: State University of New York Press.

In the fourth section of Virgil's Georgics, there is a digressive sequence about an older man. Clay demonstrates that this portion of the poem is designed to mark a transition from the erotic theme of the preceding poems to a different subject matter. Previous discussions on this poem have ignored its importance to shift theme and tone. The author takes pains to show that the senex plays a pivotal role in the Georgics.

8-150.   De Luce, J. (1989).   Ovid as an idiographic study of creativity and old age.   In T. M. Falkner & J. de Luce (Eds.), Old age in Greek and Latin literature (pp. 195-216). Albany, NY: State University of New York Press.

Continuity versus change in the writings of Ovid is the subject of this essay. De Luce speculates about whether or not creativity changes in old age. Likewise, the author wonders if poetic expression changes over time. In order to provide a tentative answer to these questions, De Luce compares and contrasts Ovid's earlier and later works. Because the Roman poet lived in exile, his poetry presents special problems, namely, trying to ascertain if exile or old age contributed to changes in his poetic output. The author believes that the best procedure for determining change over a lifespan would be to make a content analysis of the works.

8-151.   Esler, C. C. (1989).   Horace's old girls: Evolution of a topos.   In T. M. Falkner & J. de Luce (Eds.), Old age in Greek and Latin literature (pp. 172-182). Albany, NY: State University of New York Press.

The poet Horace has 3 odes to aging women. In this essay, Esler discusses their portrayal in these poetic works. The poem to Lydia chronicles her progressive decline and is very strident in its description of the woman. The ode to Chloris, in contrast, is less harsh but is uncomplimentary. The third poem is more complex, and less stereotypic. In her concluding remarks, Esler speculates that Horace's negative characterization of older women may be attributed to the cultural milieu in which he lived and wrote.

8-152. Falkner, T. M. (1989). 'Επὶ γήραος οὐδῷ: Homeric heroism, old age and the end of the Odyssey. In T. M. Falkner & J. de Luce (Eds.), Old age in Greek and Latin literature (pp. 21-67). Albany, NY: State University of New York Press.

A thorough discussion of Homer's Odyssey and old age is the subject of this essay. Falkner focuses on the Laertes episode to discuss the hero's old age. Prior to his discussion of this specific segment of the poem, the author provides the reader with a detailed background of old age in traditional societies and the formulaic elements of the "threshold of old age" in the Homeric epics. Falkner shows that a reputed loss in Homer's creative abilities is instead a change in intensity.

8-153. George, D. H. (1986). "Who is the double ghost whose head is smoke?" Women poets on aging. In K. Woodward, & M. M. Schwartz (Eds.), Memory and desire: Aging--literature--psychoanalysis (pp. 134-153). Bloomington, IN: Indiana University Press.

This analysis of contemporary female poets aged 50 to 70 from the perspective of a "daughter" who is seeking answers to basic questions about aging provides an interesting perspective. George notes that women poets treat old age in an open, irate, and challenging way. The author's psychoanalytic scrutiny of women's poetry shows a reconstruction and reevaluation of reminiscences which allow the poet to transform herself in the present.

8-154. King, H. (1989). Tithonos and Tettix. In T. M. Falkner & J. de Luce (Eds.), Old age in Greek and Latin literature (pp. 69-89). Albany, NY: State University of New York Press.

In this essay, the myth of Eos and Tithonus is studied. In that myth, Tithonus asks for immortality and receives, albeit without the benefit of agelessness. King then discusses old age within the context of this unhappy situation.

8-155. Luke, D. (1978). "How is it that you live, and what is it that you do?: The question of old age in English Romantic poetry. In S. F. Spicker, K. M.

Woodward, & D. Van Tassel (eds.), <u>Aging and the elderly: Humanistic perspectives in gerontology</u> (pp. 221-240). Atlantic Highlands, NJ: Humanities Press, Inc.

English Romantic writers often wrote of the "old man," this theme has been ignored by critics.   Until the Romantic period, the older male was strictly a comic figure.   In this essay, Luke examines the <u>senex</u> of the Romantic writers as a central, sympathetic character.   William Wordsworth and John Keats both included older males in their poetry, but they were quite different in their portrayals.   The former focuses on the spiritual element of old age while the latter depicts this stage of life as revelation of life itself.

8-156. Muller, J. (1986). Light and wisdom of the dark: Aging and language of desire in the texts of Louise Bogan. In K. Woodward, & M. M. Schwartz (Eds.), <u>Memory and desire: Aging--literature--psychoanalysis</u> (pp. 76-96). Bloomington, IN: Indiana University Press.

Careful scrutiny of Bogan's poetry within a Lacanian framework reveals the poet's search for an other to arrive at a completeness.   In her poetry, we see a continuous accommodation to the change wrought by aging.

8-157. Peyre, H. (1984). Can old age be beautiful? Or creative? Remarks of an octogenarian. In L. Porter, L. M. Porter (eds.), <u>Aging in literature</u> (pp. 149-160). Troy, MI: International Book Publishers.

This essay is a poignant overview of important literary accounts of old age and death by many of the great European writers.   Because many of Peyre's examples derive from poetry, the revered literary scholar argues for an anthology of poetry of death.

8-158. Smith, C. H. (1991). Adrienne Rich, Ruth Whitman, and their Jewish elders. <u>International Journal of Aging and Human Development</u>, <u>33</u>, 203-209.

In this study, Smith discusses 2 American poets who have written about their cultural roots.   Rich writes of her parents efforts to conceal their Jewish heritage and its effect upon her.   Ruth Whitman's poetry, however, reveals her joy at being part of the Jewish tradition.   Thus, 2 deeply felt responses to cultural traditions are represented through the medium of poetry.

8-159. Sohngen, M., & Smith R. J. (1978). Images of old age in poetry. <u>The Gerontologist</u>, <u>18</u>, 181-186.

Granger's Index of Poetry, 127 poems under the rubric of "old age," constitutes the data base for this study. Sohngen demonstrates that much of the poetry that is used in our educational systems is stereotypic. Negative depictions of the physical, emotional and social losses permeate the poetry examined. The author provides viable suggestions for using the poetry of aging in a positive and effective manner.

8-160. Trueblood, F. M. (1991). The prison of youth: Generational viewpoints in works by Gabriela Mistral and Rosario Castellenos. International Journal of Aging and Human Development, 33, 197-202.

The depiction of age in the poetry of Mistral (Chile, Nobel Prize for literature, 1945) and Castellanos (Mexico) reveals an exultation of the female self in societies that repressed women. The perspective of both poets in their later years shows common, and enduring intergenerational values.

8-161. Wilson, R. N. (1986). Review essay: For which was the first made? Poetic reflections on the last of life. The Gerontologist, 26, 457-458.

Poetic ruminations of aging are quite heterogeneous as demonstrated by judicious selections from the works of Yeats, Edmund Waller, Keats, and Sue Walker. According to Wilson, the poet has a chance at immortality while most of us can only hope to be remembered by the next 2 generations.

8-162. Woodward, K. M. (1978). Master songs of meditation: The late poems of Eliot, Pound, Stevens, and Williams. In S. F. Spicker, K. M. Woodward, & D. Van Tassel, Aging and the elderly: Humanistic perspectives in gerontology (pp. 181-202). Atlanta Highlands, NJ: Humanities Press.

Did old age produce poetic ability in the works of 4 great twentieth-century poets? An examination of the last poetic works of Eliot (The Four Quartets), Pound (Pisan Cantos), Stevens (The Rock), and Williams (Paterson V) reveals a certain creative fertility. Woodward argues that this poetry is a distinct genre with certain identifiable properties such as reflective meditation, stability, and the appearance of the wise old man. Each poet's work is analyzed and compared with reference to the properties noted.

8-163. Woodward, K. M. (1980). At last, the real distinguished thing: The late poems of Eliot, Pound, Stevens and Williams. Columbus, OH: The Ohio State University Press.

In this analysis of a single long poem in the late-life creative poetic efforts of 4 distinguished poets, Woodward seeks to place such work in a contextual framework of these author's earlier writings. This work provides insights into the nature, and the duration of creativity. Woodward notes that the 4 poets evoke a missing element in contemporary culture--the pursuit of the eternal. This volume offers significant commentary on the 4 poets under scrutiny.

8-164. Zavatsky, B. (1984). Journey through the feminine: The life review poems of William Carlos Williams. In M. Kaminsky, (Ed.), The uses of reminiscence (pp. 167-191). New York: Haworth Press.

Pertinent biographical data show that strong women played an important role in his personal development. This factor seems to have influenced the content of his life review poems because of their obvious "feminine" features. The author uses selected poetic passages to demonstrate his thesis.

9

ART

9-1. Achenbaum, W. A., & Kusnerz, P. A. (1978). Images of old age in America: 1790 to the present. Ann Arbor, MI: Institute of Gerontology, The University of Michigan/Wayne State University.

The visuals and most of the script for this book originally appeared in an exhibit with the same name as this published volume. This volume contains photographs, artwork, and other graphic displays that depict old age pictorially. The work is divided into 3 historic periods: (1) 1790-1864; (2) 1865-1934; and (3) 1935 to the present. A visual portrait of the changing attitudes toward older adults is reflected in this collection.

9-2. Berg, G., & Gadow, S. (1978). Toward more human meanings in aging: Ideals and images from philosophy and art. In S. F. Spicker, K. M. Woodward, & D. Van Tassel (Eds.), Aging and the elderly: Humanistic perspectives in gerontology (pp. 83-92). Atlantic Highlands, NJ: Humanities Press.

In this examination of the artistic expression of aging as a human experience, as opposed to a physiological, psycho-socio-cultural, economic experience, Berg and Gadow seeks to discover the significance of aging. Among the topics discussed include: (1) symbolic manifestations of the processes of aging; (2) images of the aging process; (3) personal declarations of aging; and (4) comparison of early and late artistry. A total of 7 color plates, and 1 black-

and-white plate are featured (Dorothea Lange, Cezanne, Jan van Eyck, Piet Mondrian, R. van der Weyden).

9-3. Cole, T. R. (1987). Review of The art of aging: A celebration of old age in Western art by P. McKee, and H. Kauppinen, New York: Human Sciences Press. The Gerontologist, 27, 810.

In this review, Cole is pleased to see the publication of a volume devoted to a visual characterization of aging and older adults. Nevertheless, certain flaws are noted. For one thing, art is used to sustain sociological issues, and is therefore a subservient discipline. Cole feels that this approach creates a "forced" image of old age. A preferable treatment would have art used to stimulate new insights on aging. See 9-9.

9-4. Cole, T. R., & Meyer, D. L. (1991). Aging, metaphor, and meaning: A view from cultural history. In G. M. Kenyon, J. E. Birren, and J. J. F. Schroots (Eds.), Metaphors of aging in science and the humanities (pp. 57-82). New York: Springer Publishing Company.

Although this essay deals with figurative language, 2 traditional archetypal metaphors of the ages of life, and the journey of life are represented through artistic manifestations of 2 painters--Thomas Cole (nineteenth century), and Jasper Johns (twentieth century). A thorough explication of these very different artists shows that their art reflects distinctive representation of aging. A total of 8 plates complement this study.

9-5. Covey, H. (1991). Images of older people in Western art and society. New York: Praeger Publishers.

The perception of older people through western art in various historical periods (Middle Ages, Renaissance, etc.) is the topic of this book. Covey uses historical documents and literature to buttress the claims made about the perception of older adults through the artistic medium. In addition to introductory and concluding chapters, the author discusses 5 main areas: (1) the ages of life; (2) symbolic images of older people; (3) images of older people and the family; (4) older people and sexual images; and (5) images of older people and death. This book is an interdisciplinary masterpiece. 41 black-and-white plates, and an index complement this work.

9-6. Freeman, J. T. (1976). Stamps and the students of aging. The Gerontologist, 16, 474-477.

Gerontophilately is now a recognized topical theme for stamp collectors. The theme of aging on postage stamps is frequent on international postage stamps and includes such themes as famous gerontologists, social welfare and aging, long-lived people of distinction, commemoration of older people, and so forth. Colored plates of selected stamps which contain artistic themes are featured.

9-7. Kauppinen, H. (1991). Aging in art: Beyond stereotypes. International Journal of Aging and Human Development, 33, 217-232.

In this empirical analysis of 424 artistic works dealing with old age, Kauppinen found that the pictorial representation of old age combined both positive and negative views of the final stage of life. The discussion centers on social influence and power, and sexuality. Works of art can serve a vital ancillary role in the depiction of gerontological concepts.

9-8. Kauppinen, H., & McKee, P. (1988). Old age, painting, and gerontology. The Journal of Aesthetic Education, 22(2), 87-101.

Gerontologists conceptualize old age in 2 different ways: (1) a period of decline, degradation, and deterioration; and (2) a period of growth. In this essay, Kauppinen and McKee discuss several themes of aging as depicted in various paintings: (1) life style (activity versus disengagement); (2) mental development and wisdom; and (3) intergenerational exchanges.

9-9. McKee, P., & Kauppinen, H. (1987). The art of aging: A celebration of old age in western art. New York: Human Sciences Press.

Part I of this volume contains 5 chapters on different themes of old age: (1) old age in art; (2) different ways of aging; (3) the wisdom of old age; (4) generations; and (5) the representation of old age in myths. Part II features 116 illustrations, each with a commentary. A useful "List of Illustrations" (pp. 176-184), "Bibliography" (pp. 185-187), and an "Index" (pp. 189-193) complement the text. 116 pictures are featured. See 9-3.

9-10. O'Connor, F. (1979). Albert Berne and the completion of being: Images of vitality and extinction in the last paintings of a 96-year-old man. In D. Van Tassel (Ed.), Aging, death, and the completion of being (pp. 255-289). Philadelphia: University of Pennsylvania Press.

Albert Berne (1877-1973) was an artist whose creative efforts accelerated in his final year. In a period of 162 days, Berne painted 147 canvasses. O'Connor seeks to discover in this artist's works and personal correspondence some clues to the aging psyche. A total of 16 plates (2 in color) complement this essay.

9-11.   Pritikin, R.   (1990).   Marcel Duchamp, the artist, and the social expectations of aging.   The Gerontologist, 30, 636-639.

French artist Marcel Duchamp (1887-1968) has been judged by various art critics as the best artist of the twentieth century.   Pritikin demonstrates that Duchamp's creativity and innovation continued unabated to the very end.

10

HUMOR

10-1. Barrick, A. L., Hutchinson, R. L., & Deckers, L. H. (1990). Humor, aggression, and aging. The Gerontologist, 30(5), 675-678.

154 younger and older male and females volunteered to participate in a rating of the funniness and degree of pain depicted in 38 cartoons. Results indicate that males found the cartoons funnier than females. Moreover, the female participants demonstrated an inverted U relationship in pain and funniness ratings. This study has implications for age-related differences in humor. Further research may be important for communication with older adults.

10-2. Datan, N. (1986). The last minority: Humor, old age, and marginal identity. In L. Nahemow, K. A. McCluskey-Fawcett, & P. E. McGhee (Eds.), Humor and aging (pp. 161-171). Orlando, FL: Academic Press.

According to the author, the humor of aging and ethnic humor are comparable. First, there is an imposed humor (humor by a majority about a minority). Next, the position of the "resilient underdog" allows the person to convert unpleasant realities into humor. Finally, the humor of power permits the individual to use humor to expose basic fears from the point of view of an insider.

10-3. Davies, L. J. (1977). Attitudes toward old age and aging as shown by humor. The Gerontologist, 17, 220-226.

A sample of 6 humor books yielded 363 jokes about aging and 187 about death exclusive of repeated materials (33 items). A content analysis indicated six categories of humor on aging: (1) sexuality; (2) physical; (3) social relationships; (4) mental ability; (5) age concealment; and (6) old maid/bachelor jokes. Humor related to death also included six categories: (1) dying; (2) wills and insurance; (3) tombstones; (4) funerals; (5) undertaker; and (6) life after death. Since most of the humor was negative (especially about women), a pro-active stance to combat stereotypical treatment of older adults is suggested.

10-4. Davies, L. J. (1978). Mr. Davies replies: Humor and aging: Restated. The Gerontologist, 18, 74-76.

The author agrees with Weber and Cameron (10-25) that independent raters are necessary to evaluate humor about aging. Davies disagrees about the suggestion to fight actively against ageist stereotypes in jokes.

10-5. Fry, W. F., Jr. (1976). Psychodynamics of sexual humor: Sex and the elderly. Medical Aspects of Human Sexuality, 10, 140-148.

Humor about sexuality in old age is negative and focuses on performance failures. Fry notes, however, that humor often deals with covert issues which is not openly expressed. The elements that such humor addresses are guilt and the time paradox (the realization of an encroaching loss of limited time).

10-6. Fry, W. F., Jr. (1986). Humor, physiology, and the aging process. In L. Nahemow, K. A. McCluskey-Fawcett, & P. E. McGhee (Eds.), Humor and aging (pp. 81-98). Orlando, FL: Academic Press.

Humor physiology of the co-occurring events that take place in our bodies in association with humor and its relationship to the aging process is the subject of this essay. Research in this area demonstrates that the effect of humor and mirth on the body is immediate and extensive because it stimulates the various physiological systems (cardiac, respiratory, muscular, skeletal, central nervous). Knowledge of this phenomenon has important implications in the patient-physician contact as well as the quality of life of the older adult.

10-7. Johnson, H. A. (1990). Humor as an innovative method for teaching sensitive topics. Educational Gerontology, 16, 547-559.

A recommendation to use humor in the teaching of sensitive subject matter (death, dying, suicide, grief, fear of aging) finds its justification in various psychological theories (relief, arousal, affective, liberation, and freedom) of humor. The introduction of humor into a clinical setting serves to reduce anxiety, to function as a coping mechanism for caregiver and patient alike. The educational benefits of humor include an augmentation in the retention of materials, and increase in student ratings of instructors.

10-8. Loeb, M., & Wood, V. (1986). Epilogue: A nascent idea for an Eriksonian model of humor. In L. Nahemow, K. A. McCluskey-Fawcett, & P. E. McGhee (Eds.), Humor and aging (pp. 279-284).   Orlando, FL: Academic Press.

After the death of Martin Loeb, co-author Wood finished the incomplete essay for this volume. In this overview, an Eriksonian model of humor is sketched out.   Erikson's 8 stages of human development are reviewed with special attention to the role of humor in each period.

10-9. Lorenz, C. A., & Vecsey, C. (1986). Hopi ritual clowns and values in the Hopi life span. In L. Nahemow, K. A. McCluskey-Fawcett, & P. E. McGhee (Eds.), Humor and aging (pp. 199-220). Orlando, FL: Academic Press.

Cross-cultural perspectives on humor and aging can provide interesting insights into this phenomenon. A part of the culture of the Hopi Indians of Arizona involves ritual clowning.   This aspect of Hopi culture involves important psychological, religious, cognitive, and societal functions. Hopi Indians do not pay attention to age per se unless an older person is unhealthy. The latter become objects of scorn and derision in this culture as symbolized by the mocking rituals of the clowns. In the clown rituals, unhealthy older people are objects of scorn in recognition of the fact that they are no longer considered to be real Hopis.

10-10. McGhee, P. E. (1986). Humor across the life span: Sources of developmental change and individual differences. In L. Nahemow, K. A. McCluskey-Fawcett, & P. E. McGhee (Eds.), Humor and aging (pp. 27-51). Orlando, FL: Academic Press.

A number of factors influence humor development in human beings (genetics, temperament and personality, environmental influences). Although McGhee's research on universals in the development of humor focuses on childhood, a period when trends in humor acquisition and development reflect cognitive changes, it is possible that disparagement theory and cognitive theories will provide insights into the development of humor across the entire life span.

10-11. McGhee, P. E., Bell, N. J., & Duffey, N. S. (1986). Generational differences in humor and correlates of humor development. In L. Nahemow,

K. A. McCluskey-Fawcett, & P. E. McGhee (Eds.), Humor and aging (pp. 253-263). Orlando, FL: Academic Press.

2 exploratory studies were carried out to determine the relationship of 2 groups of adults to determine their personal joking and humor compared to that of their parents. The first test involved 446 undergraduate students (205 male, 241 female). Each subject was asked to respond to a questionnaire which included questions about humor (initiation, responsiveness, parent's humor patterns). A second study with the same questionnaire was carried out with a group of older women (27 subjects, ages 60s to 80s). A comparison of the results indicates a high correspondence between current social assertiveness and interest and enjoyment of humor. Likewise, there is a correlation of children's humor development stimulated by the parent of the same sex. Patterns of humor appear to be stable across the lifespan.

10-12. Nahemow, L. (1986). Humor as a data base for the study of aging. In L. Nahemow, K. A. McCluskey-Fawcett, & P. E. McGhee (Eds.), Humor and aging (pp. 1-26). Orlando, FL: Academic Press.

The use of humor as a source of information on aging is scrutinized methodically in this essay. Nahemow reviews and discusses the implications of the major psychological theories designed to encompass humor and aging. The theories include: Drive reduction theory; cognitive theory; psychoanalytic theory; disposition theory; and ecological theory. The author states that what is and is not humorous reveals much about attitudes and fears.

10-13. Nahemow, L., McCluskey-Fawcett, K. A., & McGhee, P. E. (Eds.), Humor and aging. Orlando, FL: Academic Press.

The 16 studies in this anthology deal with distinct aspects of humor and aging from psychological, sociological, developmental, and philosophical perspectives. Author and subject indices complement this collection.

10-14. Nahemow, L., & Rayman, A. (1986). Performers' views of humor and aging. In L. Nahemow, K. A. McCluskey-Fawcett, & P. E. McGhee (Eds.), Humor and aging (pp. 265-277). Orlando, FL: Academic Press.

An interview with 40 comedic performers yielded interesting results about actual performance that correlated well with experimental testing and theoretical assumptions. The choice of materials used by comedians was influenced by the age of the target audience. The authors urge further research to measure objectively what causes people to laugh.

10-15. O'Connell, W. E. (1968). Humor and death. Psychological Reports, 22, 391-402.

An empirical analysis of humorous attitude and attitude toward one's own death is the subject of this article.   Kalish's Attitude on Social Issues Test and O'Connell's Story Test (with 12 items on high- and low-death themes) were administered to 96 college seniors. The purpose of this experiment was to shed light on Freudian humor.   O'Connell found a number of correlations, fears, perils, and anxieties about death that merit further research.

10-16. Palmore, E. (1971). Attitudes toward aging shown by humor. The Gerontologist, 11, 181-186.

The 10 most popular humor books provided 264 jokes about aging and older adults.   The themes of this humor included: (1) longevity; (2) physical appearance; (3) obsolescence; (4) sexuality; (5) age concealment; (6) old maid; (7) retirement; (8) mental acuity; (9) state of felicity; and (10) death. More than 50% of the jokes were negative. In particular, humor about women and age was more negative than jokes related to men and old age.

10-17. Palmore, E. (1978). Dr. Palmore replies. The Gerontologist, 18, 76.

In a brief reply (see 10-25), Palmore agrees that independent rating of humor is important. Ageist humor, however, ought to be as equally unacceptable as sexist and racist jokes.

10-18. Palmore, E. B. (1986). Attitudes toward aging shown by humor: A review. In L. Nahemow, K. A. McCluskey-Fawcett, & P. E. McGhee (Eds.), Humor and aging (pp. 101-119). Orlando, FL: Academic Press.

A content analysis of humor about older adults provides a means of evaluating unconscious attitudes toward this group. In his review of the available research on this topic, Palmore shows that a majority of the humor about older people and the aging process is negative. Themes include longevity, physical and mental ability, appearance, sexuality, and age concealment.   Much more research needs to be carried out before any definitive statements about this data source can be made.

10-19. Richman, J. (1977). The foolishness and wisdom of age: Attitudes toward the elderly as reflected in jokes. The Gerontologist, 17, 210-219.

100 jokes about older adults were compared to 160 humorous tales about children. 7 negative themes about old age (age concealment, physical appeal,

an undesirable state, physical/mental decline, sexual decline, death, non-conformity to age-determined tasks) and three positive themes (affirmation of life, sexuality, inherent value) were chronicled. More negative attitudes were found in the humor about older people than in that about children. This study argues against Palmore's conclusions (10-16).

10-20. Richman, J. (1978). Dr. Richman replies. The Gerontologist, 18, 77-79.

The author responds to the Weber and Cameron (10-25) critique of 5 specific jokes in his 1977 study. Richman defends humor as a worthy source for investigation about attitudes toward older adults.

10-21. Rosenberg, E. (1986). Humor and the death system: An investigation of funeral directors. In L. Nahemow, K. A. McCluskey-Fawcett, & P. E. McGhee (Eds.), Humor and aging (pp. 173-198). Orlando, FL: Academic Press.

In this sociological and thanatological study, the undertaking profession is examined because of its intimate association with death. Interviews with 9 funeral directors were conducted with a set of 9 questions concerning humor and their profession. The humor of this profession consists of anecdotes and spontaneous wit rather than a repertoire of stock jokes. The author believes that more research into this topic is required, e.g., the humor of obituary writers or casket manufacturers. Moreover, there is a need to alter investigational strategies for better reporting of data.

10-22. Schaie, K. W., & Cicirelli, V. G. (1976). Age differences in humor comprehension and appreciation in old age. Journal of Gerontology, 31, 577-582.

In this empirical study, 3 age groups (50-59, 60-69, 70-79) were presented with a total of 24 jokes (12 involved Piagetian concepts of mass, weight, and volume; 12 did not). Results of the experiment indicated that for both kinds of jokes, appreciation increased with age and comprehension decreased with age. The cognitive perceptual theory of humor in old age finds support in this test since a correlation between ability level and cognitive requirements of the joke exists.

10-23. Seltzer, M. M. (1986). Timing: The significant common variable in both humor and aging. In L. Nahemow, K. A. McCluskey-Fawcett, & P. E. McGhee (Eds.), Humor and aging (pp. 121-137). Orlando, FL: Academic Press.

In her discussion of timing and its relationship to humor and aging, Seltzer considers the psychological and social dimensions of the phenomenon. It appears that certain humor about aging is timeless as evidenced by its appearance in earlier literature (Greek and Latin works, Chaucer, and Shakespeare). Nevertheless, there is an element of humor that changes in response to the social situation and current issues. Intergenerational conflicts and tensions are also documented in humor. This essay raises many questions that might be the topic of future research.

10-24. Thorson, J. A. (1985). A funny thing happened on the way to the morgue: Some thoughts on humor and death, and taxonomy of humor associated with death. Death Studies, 9, 201-216.

Death and humor have received little attention. In this study, Thorson examines this form of humor and establishes 10 basic categories: (1) Body humor (undertakers, funerals, burial, necrophilia, cannibalism); (2) personality (death scenes and last words, memories of the deceased, suicide and murder, gallows humor, personification of death). Such humor functions as a defense mechanism and social salve.

10-25. Weber, T., & Cameron, P. (1978). Comment: Humor and aging--a response. The Gerontologist, 18, 73-76.

In this review of 3 previous studies on humor and aging (10-3, 10-16, 10-19), the authors question the reliability of assessing the attitude contained in a joke because so many variables are involved (speaker, hearer, situational elements, delivery). It is important to determine the functions of such humor before labeling specific jokes as negative.

11

CARTOONS

11-1. Ansello, E. F. (1986). Male-female long-term relationships as a source of humor. In L. Nahemow, K. A. McCluskey-Fawcett, & P. E. McGhee (Eds.), Humor and aging (pp. 233-244). Orlando, FL: Academic Press.

In this study, Ansello examined 90 newspaper cartoons and comic strips published from 1979 to 1984 to determine the types of humor to be found in long-term male-female interactions. Antagonism, catharsis, shared intimacy, and accommodation to gender role changes emerged as the 4 major categories. Since cartoons are a reflective medium, much can be determined about mid-life and late-life relationships. The author argues for additional study of this database.

11-2. Posner, J. (1975). Dirty old women: Buck Brown's cartoons. Canadian Review of Sociology and Anthropology, 12(4, Part I), 471-473.

Buck Brown has drawn a series of single-panel cartoons for Playboy magazine which features a "dirty old woman" labeled "granny." In counterpoint to the archetypal "dirty old man," this cartoon demeans women because it reinforces stereotypes about older women's sexuality as abhorrent creatures. Posner offers a Freudian interpretation of this element from popular culture.

11-3. Sheppard, A. (1981). Response to cartoons and attitudes toward aging. Journal of Gerontology, 36, 122-126.

253 college-age students (107 males, 146 females) rated 60 cartoons related to aging gleaned from popular magazines. This study sought to determine what kinds of cartoons were perceived as humorous as a way of determining attitudes toward aging. Sheppard failed to find a correlation between attitudes toward cartoons about aging and attitudes.

11-4. Smith, M. D. (1979). The portrayal of elders in magazine cartoons. The Gerontologist, 19, 408-412.

In a content analysis of 2,217 cartoons selected from 8 popular magazines, 95 (4.3%) contained older adults. 3 elements were considered: presence of older adults, gender, and positive or negative depiction of older people. In their infrequent appearances in cartoons, older adults are usually negative. Smith suggests that such humor may be a mechanism for our society to face aging.

12

GREETING CARDS

12-1. Demos, V., & Jache, A. (1981, September 22). Return to sender--please! Woman's Day, pp. 20-21.

This brief note summarizes observations made by the authors in their research project on birthday cards (see 12-2).

12-2. Demos, V., & Jache, A. (1981). When you care enough: An analysis of attitudes toward aging in humorous birthday cards. The Gerontologist, 21, 209-215.

Content analysis of 195 humorous birthday cards revealed a predominantly negative depiction of aging. Age-related themes included physical and mental characteristics, age concealment, age boundaries, aging as a process, aging as a state of mind, an experience of others, and aging as a mortal concern.

12-3. Dillon, K. M., & Jones, B. S. (1981). Attitudes toward aging portrayed by birthday cards. International Journal of Aging and Human Development, 13(1), 79-84.

240 greeting cards were examined in this study. Results showed that 6 themes related to aging the most frequent: (1) loss (senses, physical health, mental health, sexuality); (2) age concealment; (3) sympathy or respect for older adults;

(4) situational improvement attributed to age; (5) age as a mental attitude; and (6) not appearing to be one's true age.   The authors speculate on the psychological effects of humorous greeting cards.

12-4.   Huyck, M. H., & Duchon, J.   (1986).   Over the miles: Coping, communicating, and commiserating through age-theme greeting cards.   In L. Nahemow, K. A. McCluskey-Fawcett, & P. E. McGhee (Eds.), Humor and aging (pp. 139-159).   Orlando, FL: Academic Press.

In this empirical study, 32 age-theme greeting cards were selected as stimuli. 58 subjects (ages 23-70) were asked the following questions: (1) The intention of the message of the card; (2) the reaction of the recipient to receiving the card; and (3) the reaction of the respondents themselves to receiving such a card.   The responses were tabulated for the following variables: (1) coping style; (2) aggressive components; (3) respondent demographic information; and (4) data concerning the relationship between sender and receiver.   The researchers concluded that their study supported Freud's contentions about the use of humor to express concealed sentiments. Huyck and Duchon further argue that this form of humor is a coping strategy, but they note that more research is necessary.

13

ADVICE TO
OLDER ADULTS

13-1. Arluke, A., Levin, J., & Suchwalko, J. (1984). Sexuality and romance in advice books for the elderly. The Gerontologist, 24, 415-419.

A total of 65 advice books for older adults were reviewed to determine romantic and sexual content. 25% of the sample was published before 1970, the remaining 75% appeared after 1970. Some attitudinal improvement concerning advice on sexual activity in these publications has occurred since 1970. Nevertheless, romance (remarriage and dating) continues to be disparaged.

13-2. Gaitz, C. M., & Scott, J. (1975). Analysis of letters to "Dear Abby" concerning old age. The Gerontologist, 15, 47-50.

2 sets of letters written to the newspaper column "Dear Abby" by or about older adults in late 1973 were analyzed for their content. Primary concerns of older adults include loneliness, rejection, personal relations, sexuality, and search for another spouse. Younger writers are concerned about parental care and related economic aspects. These findings correspond to the problem areas cited by gerontologists and mental health care workers.

14

ADVERTISING

14-1. Gantz, W., Gartenber, H. M., & Rainbow, C. K. (1980). Approaching invisibility: The portrayal of the elderly in magazine advertisements. Journal of Communication, 30, 56-60.

7 national magazines for the year 1977 produced a total of 6,785 advertisements. An analysis of this data base showed that only 404 (5.9%) featured older adults. Moreover, of 17,838 people who appeared in the sample, only 551 (3.1%) were older persons. Finally, men outnumbered women in the total sample by a margin of 3 to 1. The paucity of older adults in the advertisements suggests their marginal societal role.

14-2. Hollenshead, C., & Ingersoll, B. (1982). Middle-aged and older women in print advertisements. Educational Gerontology, 8, 25-41.

In this content analysis of 3 types of periodicals (Time, Good Housekeeping, Journal of American Medical Association), 6 random samples of each publication for the years 1967 and 1977 were selected. Few examples of older women, negative or positive, in advertisements occurred (30 of 3,482 advertisements). Elements considered in this study included frequency of appearance of older women, products featured, and setting. Some positive transformations in the depiction of older women occurred in Time and Good Housekeeping.

14-3. Kvasnicka, B., Beymer, B., & Perloff, R. M. (1982). Portrayals of the elderly in magazine advertisements. Journalism Quarterly, 54, 656-658.

An examination of 4 national magazines (Better Homes & Gardens, McCalls, Readers Digest, and TV Guide) with a high readership among older adults, and 4 specialized magazines (Fifty Plus, Modern Maturity, Retirement Life, and Retirement Living) from the year 1980 were surveyed to determine the number of older adults featured in advertisements. 8% (168 of 2,108 ads) of the national magazines featured older people while 77.2% (561 of 727 ads) were featured in the specialized publications. The latter depicted older adults more favorably than did the national publications. This research project was a followup to item 14-1 above.

14-4. Smith, M. C. (1976). Portrayal of the elderly in prescription drug advertising: A pilot study. The Gerontologist, 16, 329-334.

Medical Economics and Geriatrics provided the data base for this content analysis on the depiction of older adults in prescription drug advertisements in 1974. 132 older people appeared in the advertisements. Visible depiction of older adults in the 2 publications portrayed older people as active. The verbal descriptions, however, were negative. Such advertising may induce negative stereotypes of older patients and affect physicians' attitudes.

15

MAGAZINES

15-1. Duncan, K. J. (1963). Modern society's attitudes toward aging.
Geriatrics, 18, 629-635.

A review of 2 major indexes to periodical literature (Poole's Index of Periodical Literature, and The Reader's Guide to Periodical Literature) were examined for the period 1887 to 1963 to determine the frequency of articles on aging and attitudinal shifts on aging and aging as a personal problem. 50 years prior to this study, 4 themes predominated (pensions, economic aspects, housing, and adjustment to aging). At the time the research for this article was carried out, these same topics continued to be of interest. However, several additional subjects also became prominent (recreation, diet, exercise, and age deferment). Age as a topic of concern continues to grow.

15-2. Kaiser, S. B., & Chandler, P. W. (1988). Audience response to appearance codes: Old-age imagery in the media. The Gerontologist, 28, 692-694.

A survey of 55 older adults (average age 69.3) from northern California was conducted to determine their reaction to eleven 8"x10" framed, color photographs of older people (celebrities and anonymous models) selected from popular magazines. The study sought to determine the reaction to the appearance codes of the people depicted in this form of popular literature. The researchers suggest that diversity in appearance is a desirable strategy to present a balanced view of this group.

15-3. Kent, K. E. M., & Shaw, P. (1980). Age in Time: A study of stereotyping. The Gerontologist, 20, 598-601.

In this study of named individuals in all issues of Time magazine for 1978, 81 of 599 people were identified by age. Only 11.1% of people over 60 were identified stereotypically (versus 8.5% for those under 60). Women are more likely to be identified by age, however. The authors conclude that little ageism exists in Time.

15-4. Loetterle, B. C. (1985). Ageless prose: A study of media projected images of aging as reflected in content analysis of magazines for older persons (Doctoral dissertation, City University of New York, 1984). Dissertation Abstracts International, 45, 2220A.

A content analysis of 2 major magazines (Modern Maturity, 50 Plus) designed for older adults to determine the changes and continuities in the depiction of older adults. A total of 12 major categories (and 137 subcategories) were examined: Leisure time; realities of aging; retirement; value orientation, religion and spirituality; daily living; health; economics; residential patterns; part time work, second career; volunteer activity; family; and coping mechanisms. The 2 magazines address healthy older adults with no visible indications of aging until they are 75. These 2 publications project a positive image of old age which helps to diminish this society's ageism.

15-5. Martel, U. M. (1968). Age-sex roles in American magazine fiction (1890-1955). In B. L. Neugarten (ed.), Middle age and aging: A reader in social psychology (pp. 47-57). Chicago: University of Chicago Press.

A selective review of popular magazine fiction (American, Cosmopolitan, Ladies' Home Journal, Saturday Evening Post) during a 65 year period constitutes a data base to measure change and stability in age and sex roles in this period. The author warns on several occasions that the world of the magazine is unlikely to be realistic. With this admonition in mind, Martel notes significant changes in intergenerational contacts, and the significance of age, e.g., wisdom shifts to obsolescence.

15-6. Murphy, J. E. (1980). The image of old age and the elderly in preindustrial America: A content analysis of selected eighteenth and nineteenth century magazines (Southern Illinois University, Carbondale, 1979). Dissertation Abstracts International, 40, 4765A.

An examination of the position and role of older adults in fiction and non-fiction in the important magazines published between 1741 and 1865 revealed that a quarter of the magazines had references to aging and older people in poems, short stories, and non-fiction essays. Most references were brief and peripheral. A decade by decade analysis shows a shift from negative to neutral to positive by 1865. The latter finding runs counter to theories about modernization and industrialization and the societal role of older adults.

15-7. Range, J., & Vinovskis, M. A. (1981). Images of elderly in popular magazines: A content analysis of Littell's Living Age, 1845-1882. Social Science History, 5, 123-170.

A sample of 293 stories published in Littell's Living Age for a 38 year period from 1845-1882 was used to assess trends in the depiction of older adults in the past century. The authors state that older adults tended not to be major protagonists. However, the characterization of older characters was not increasingly negative in the time frame examined. Range and Vinovskis argue in favor of a content analysis approach to this type of research, and they include a useful appendix (pp. 157-165) of 82 points considered in their own research.

15-8. Schuerman, L. E., Eden, D. Z., & Peterson, D. A. (1977). Older people in women's periodical fiction. Educational Gerontology, 2, 227-251.

216 fictional stories selected from 108 issues of nine well-known women's magazines were surveyed. Results of this study showed that older adults were neither underrepresented nor in marginal roles. Second, older adults in this sample of fiction were more often depicted in a favorable light. Next, older people in these stories fail to reflect the statistical reality of the actual older population of the U.S. Finally, the fictional characters reflect the readership of the periodicals sampled.

15-9. Wang, C. (1988). LEAR'S Magazine "For the woman who wasn't born yesterday": A critical review. The Gerontologist, 28, 600-601.

A critical review of the first issue of Lear's magazine points out that this periodical focuses on women from the highest socio-economic strata. In this sense, the publication ignores minority women who live in poverty. Moreover, the inclusion of advertisements for alcohol, tobacco, and cosmetic products is questioned. Nevertheless, some features on finances, volunteerism, and intergenerational contact are viewed favorably.

16

NEWSPAPERS

16-1. Buchholtz, M., & Bynum, J. (1982). Newspaper presentation of America's aged: A content analysis of image and role. The Gerontologist, 22, 83-88.

1,703 stories about older adults in 2 daily newspapers (The Daily Oklahoman, The New York Times) were analyzed for the years 1970 and 1978. Results showed that a majority of the stories in the total sample were neutral in their depiction of images of older adults. In the rest of the data base, positive articles exceeded negative ones by a 2:1 margin. Only 11.1% of the stories dealt with issues compared to event-oriented articles. The authors recommend more coverage of trends rather than events.

16-2. Macdonald, R. (1973). Content analysis of perceptions of aging as represented by the news media. The Gerontologist, 13 (special issue), 103.

Stories about aging were clipped from an unidentified midwest newspaper for a 3 month period for 2 time periods (1973 and 1963). The results show that the major categories of stories (human interest, legislative action, biological issues and social issues) were similar in the 2 time frames.

16-3. Wass, H., Almerico, G. M., Campbell, P. V., & Tatum, J. L. (1984). Presentation of the elderly in the Sunday news. Educational Gerontology, 10, 335-348.

A sample of 1,041 articles from 254 Sunday issues of twenty-two daily papers (which represented high, medium, and low circulation) from 1983 showed that .87% of the stories dealt with aging and older adults.   Event articles outnumbered issue-oriented stories. Large urban papers included more stories on older adults in more active roles. As subjects of a story, men outnumbered v'omen. The authors conclude that more coverage is necessary.

16-4.   Wass, H., Hawkins, L. V., Kelly, E. B., Magners, C. R., & McMorrow, A. M. (1985). The elderly in the Sunday papers: 1963-1983. Educational Gerontology, 11, 29-39.

In order to make a qualitative and quantitative assessment of aging materials in Florida newspapers, a sample of 11 Sunday newspapers from 3 circulation groups (metropolitan, large and small newspapers) was used. The procedure consisted of selecting 12 issues per year (1963-1983). A measurement was made of the amount of material devoted to aging (actual number of square inches). A change from 1/2% to 3/4% occurred between 1963 and 1983. Even though there is an ever-increasing number of older adults who live in Florida, the newspapers failed to reflect this phenomenon. Most age-related articles dealt with males. The authors recommend comparable studies in other states with large numbers of older adults especially the retirement states of Arizona and California. This study shows that age-related articles have not increased in the 20-year period under review. More coverage, especially of older women, is needed.

17

HISTORY

17-1. Achenbaum, W. A. (1978). Old age in the new land: The American experience since 1790. Baltimore, MD: The Johns Hopkins University Press.

The historical dimensions of aging in the U.S. help to explain how we have arrived at our current situation. Achenbaum has divided his book into three separate parts. The first section ("Changing perceptions of the Aged's Roles in Nineteenth-Century America") notes that old age had positive connotations in our early history. From 1865 to 1914, however, written accounts of attitudes toward older people and old age became more negative. In the second section of this monograph ("The Demographic and Socioeconomic Dimensions of Old Age"), Achenbaum focuses on the factual, demographic side of aging in America to determine the actual situation of older people in society until 1914. The somewhat surprising conclusion is that popular perceptions of older people continued to be relatively positive despite emerging demographic and social shifts. The final part of this book ("Contemporary Old Age in Historical Perspective") documents the post World War I view of old age as a social problem. The cause of this shift derives both from cultural assumptions and actual societal demograhic transformations. The enactment of the Social Security Act and its impact on older adults is discussed in some detail. Finally, the status of old age since the inception of this legislation is reviewed. In his conclusion, Achenbaum speculates on future directions of aging in America. A selected bibliography and an index complement this work. A knowledge of the historical trends that influenced contemporary attitudes toward growing old in this country is essential to an informed understanding of how and why the media depict older people and old age in the late twentieth century.

17-2. Cole, T. R. (1983). The "enlightened" view of aging: Victorian morality in a new key. Hastings Center Report, 13, 34-40.

In an effort to understand the newly emergent prejudice of ageism, Cole traces its historical roots to Victorian morality which stated that those who lived an appropriate life style free of debauchery would live to a healthy old age. The result was a dualism which with a positive pole (the myth of healthy self-reliance), and a negative pole (fear of, and hostility against old age). The latter came about because of the realization that living a clean and healthy life did not always guarantee a healthy old age. Today's ageism, according to Cole, has revived the earlier nineteenth century mythology of older people as a healthy, engaged, and self-reliant group.

17-3. Covey, H. C. (1988). Historical terminology used to represent older people. The Gerontologist, 28, 292-297.

Terminology to refer to aging and to older adults was traced historically by consulting documents such as the Oxford English Dictionary and other sources. An examination of these words and phrases reflect how older people and the aging process are perceived at a given time. Covey concludes that pejorative terms for older adults have increased since the latter part of the 19th century. Moreover, negative characterization of older women in the lexicon has a longer history than that for men. This situation derives in part from the historical depiction of older women as witches.

17-4. Fischer, D. H. (1978). Growing old in America. Expanded edition. London: Oxford University Press.

This history of old age in America offers a differing perspective on this topic from that of Achenbaum (see 17-1). Chapter 1 ("The Exaltation of Age in Early America, 1607-1820") points out that in the early history of the U.S., older people enjoyed a relatively high status as indicated by a variety of non-traditional documentation. In the second chapter ("The Revolution in Age Relations, 1770-1820"), Fischer points out that society's attitudes toward old age were beginning to change, e.g., mandatory retirement laws, patterns of age preference contained in the national census, etc. The following chapter ("The Cult of Youth in Modern America, 1770-1970") notes that as old age became a more common phenomenon, this stage of life was viewed much more negatively. The author documents a growing wave of ageism that reaches its peak in the present. The fourth chapter ("Old Age Becomes a Social Problem,

1909-1970") reviews the factors that lead this country to regard old age as a "problem." In the final chapter ("A Thought for the Future"), Fischer hypothesizes about future directions for aging and older adults in this society. A new and valuable bibliographic essay, appendices, and an index complement this expanded and revised volume on the history of aging in the U.S.

17-5. Freeman, J. T. (1979). Aging: Its history and literature. New York: Human Sciences Press.

Freeman provides the reader with a valuable historical overview of aging in 4 well-written chapters: (1) The history of gerocomy, gerontology, and geriatrics; (2) 100 significant works on aging, old age, and the aged; (3) the historiology of gerontology's historiographers: A classified bibliography 1900-1975; and (4) a classified list of journals on aging, old age, and the aged to 1975. A Subject Index and a Name Index complement this useful reference work.

17-6. Haber, C. (1983). Beyond sixty-five: The dilemma of old age in America's past. New York: Cambridge University Press.

This historical account of old age in America is intended to examine the scientific classificatory schemes of old age through America's history. Such classifications were sociological, biological or institutional in their origins. Among the topics covered are: (1) the classification of age; (2) aging in the colonial period; (3) nineteenth-century perceptions and realities of old age; (4) medical categorization of old age; (5) institutionalization of older people; and (6) the relationship of pensionable age to employability. This informative volume explains the origin of present day classification of older people.

17-7. Hareven, T. K. (1979). The last stage: Historical adulthood and old age. In D. D. Van Tassel (Ed.), Aging, death, and the completion of being (pp. 165-189). Philadelphia: University of Pennsylvania Press.

The history of aging is the subject of this enlightening essay. Hareven reviews the shifting views of old age in U.S. history. Longevity has, in effect, created a new developmental stage of life that must be examined and understood. Among the topics discussed are the historical perspective of this notion, work life and productivity, and family orientation and functions. An adequate understanding of old age in contemporary society must rely on a historical sense of this notion and the factors that shaped our current attitudes.

17-8. Premo, T. L. (1983). Women growing old in the new republic: Personal responses to old age, 1785-1835 (Doctoral dissertation, University of Cincinnati, 1983). Dissertation Abstracts International, 44, 1797A.

Women's personal response to aging in the 50 year period following the American Revolution is the subject of this dissertation. Premo examines the diaries and letters of 142 women written between 1785 and 1835 as a data base. Among her findings, the author notes that older women depended upon male members of the family for financial support. Moreover, older women became models of virtue and sought support in religion. This study questions the contention that old people lost esteem after the American Revolution.

17-9. Stannard, D. E. (1977). The Puritan way of death. New York: Oxford University Press.

In this study of the Puritan notion of death, Stannard examines this concept of death in the Western tradition. In this study, the author reviews Puritan culture, death and childhood, death and dying, death and burial, and death and decline. In a lengthy epilogue, Stannard discusses the American way of death with its current manifestations of concealment and evasion.

17-10. Stearns, P. N. (1978). Toward historical gerontology. Journal of Interdisciplinary History, 8, 737-746.

In this review of Fischer's Growing old in America Stearns discusses the emerging area of generational history. 3 deficiencies in Fischer's monograph are important to note: (1) a failure to support the historical periodization used in the book; (2) omission of a definition of "old age"; and (3) reliance on secondary sources to describe the lives of older adults. Though very critical in its scope, this review manages to point out areas for future study. See 17-4.

17-11. Stearns, P. N. (1980). Old women: Some historical observations. Journal of Family History, 5, 44-57.

Little attention has been paid to older women by historians. For this reason, Stearns seeks to rectify this situation with this seminal essay. Among the issues discussed are: (1) women's longevity rate compared to men; (2) reasons for a woman's greater ability to cope with old age; (3) the role of religion in old age; (4) additional strategies employed by women to deal with their aging.

18

FILM

18-1. Butsch, R., & Baron, A. (1980). Reviewing the reviews: A note--the portrayal of elderly in films and reviews. The Gerontologist, 20, 602-603.

An examination of 15 reviews of 3 successful films with older protagonists (Harold and Maude, Harry and Tonto, and The Sunshine Boys) provides some insights into the treatment of old age. Film reviewers are accurate in their description of the characters in the films, yet these same critics fail to call attention to the unrealistic nature of the depictions of the older personages. Baron and Baron take film critics to task for their failure to act as social critics and to comment on old age and its implications in this society.

18-2. Erikson, E. H. (1979). Reflections on Dr. Borg's life cycle. In D. Van Tassel (Ed.) Aging, death, and the completion of being (pp. 29-68). Philadelphia: University of Pennsylvania Press.

In this commentary on Ingmar Bergman's Wild Strawberries, Erikson comments on the developmental stages through which the film's protagonist Dr. Isak Borg passes. The utilization of Bergman's famous film as a means of explicating Erikson's own theory of the human life cycle is imaginative and helpful. The second section of this essay focuses on the latter stages of the human life cycle which include integrity versus despair, disgust, and ultimately wisdom.

18-3. Lydon, M. (1986). L'Eden Cinema: Aging and imagination in Marguerite Duras. In K. Woodward, & M. M. Schwartz (Eds.), Memory and desire: Aging--literature--psychoanalysis (pp. 154-167). Bloomington, IN: Indiana University Press.

In this essay, Lydon traces the career of dramatist and film writer Marguerite Duras who was born in French Indo-China (now Vietnam). The author comments on Duras's relationship with her mother. Lydon discusses Duras's cinematographic career and how she acquired strength and power as she grew older.

18-4. Stoddard, K. (1980). The image of the aging woman in American film, 1930-1980 (Ph.D. Dissertation, University of Maryland, College Park, 1980). Dissertation Abstracts International, 41, 2663-2664-A.

A decade-by-decade analysis of older women in American film from 1930 to 1980 reflects changes in sex roles. The power of film to reflect reality and lend credibility to a prevailing creed is documented in popular film. Since the 1970s films have mirrored society's belief that a woman's only legitimate choice is maternity. Rather, aging women are depicted with a wide range of possibilities as contributing members of this society.

18-5. Trojan, J. (1980). Film portraits of aging men. Media and Methods, 16, 20-21, 42-44.

In this essay, 2 groups of 3 films about aging are discussed. The first group (Best Boy, Grandpa, Murita Cycles) deal with families and their relationships with older relatives. The second group of films (Home to Stay, Portrait of Grandpa Doc, Gandy Dancer) portray grandfathers who exercise considerable influence over their grandchildren.

19

MUSIC

19-1. Albertson, J. K. (1990). Old age in American sheet music. The Gerontologist, 30, 706.

In this letter to the editor, Albertson disagrees with the legitimacy of the thematic category "Fear of Old Age" established by Cohen and Kruschwitz (see 19-4).

19-2. Beckerman, M. B. (1990). Leoš Janáček and "the late style" in music. The Gerontologist, 30, 632-635.

This Czech musician (1854-1928) maintained his creativity and productivity until his death. Beckerman assesses Janáček's depiction of aging in his late operatic works, the composer's personal assessment. The notion of a creative artist's "late style," or period of integration of all previous work is disputed in this instance.

19-3. Cohen, E. S., & Kruschwitz, A. L. (1990a). Cohen and Kruschwitz reply. The Gerontologist, 30, 706.

In this response to Albertson (see 19-1), Cohen and Kruschwitz state that real fears (abandonment, poverty, and physical decline) are contained in popular sheet music.

19-4.   Cohen, E. S., & Kruschwitz, A. L.   (1990b).   Old age in America represented in nineteenth and twentieth century popular sheet music.   The Gerontologist, 30, 345-354.

The lyrics and cover art of more than 300 samples of American popular sheet music published from 1830 to 1980 were examined.   6 thematic categories were studied: (1) physical attributes; (2) sex and romance; (3) growing old together; (4) filial obligations; (5) youth versus old age; and (6) fear of aging.   These scholars note that recurring negative themes predominate.   A useful sheet music bibliography complements this essay.   See 19-1, 19-3.

19-5.   Kelley, C. E.   (1983).   Ageism in popular song: A rhetorical analysis of American popular song lyrics, 1964-1973 (Doctoral dissertation, University of Oregon, 1982).   Dissertation Abstracts International, 43, 2830A.

An analysis of popular music for a 10-year period (1964-1973) reveals a view of aging and older people that is essentially negative.   Many of the songs studied reveal a prevailing ageism.   Kelley suggests that as this generation ages, its members are likely to be victimized by the prejudice spawned in its wake.

19-6.   Leitner, M. J.   (1983).   The representation of aging in pop/rock music of the 1960s and '70s.   Activities, Adaptation and Aging, 4, 49-53.

A content analysis of 9 popular songs revealed that the themes of solitude and sadness of old age permeated most of the selections.   The influence of popular music in the formation of teenage and young adult attitudes toward older adults may be significant.

20

ORAL HISTORY

20-1. Blythe, R. (1979). The view from winter: Reflections on old age. New York: Harcourt Brace, Jovanovich.

Recorded in this book are conversations with the inhabitants of an old English village. Each of its 9 sections contains the reminiscences of the older people who dwell in this town. An introductory section precedes the actual recollections of the people. This book evokes the earlier part of twentieth-century England and allows the reader unique insights into some very frank personal experiences.

20-2. Butler, R. N. (1963). The life review: An interpretation of reminiscence in the aged. Psychiatry, 26, 65-76.

This now classic essay hypothesizes a universal incidence of a life review by older adults. The process of life review is a mechanism that allows the older person to assess, reorganize, reintegrate, and give meaning to an individual's life. This process may be creative or destructive in certain instances. Case histories, references to literary manifestations of life review, and recommendations about dealing with this normally occurring activity are discussed in detail.

20-3. Butler, R. N. (1974). Successful aging and the role of the life review. Journal of the American Geriatrics Society, 22, 529-535.

Life review, and life review group therapy may serve as effective therapeutic aids for older adults. The former refers to obtaining an extensive autobiography from older adults. These reminiscences involve several important functions: (1) a summation of an individual's life work; (2) transmission of important family history to the next generation; and (3) the resolution of psychological conflicts. The latter involves age-integrated groups of 8 to 10 people (ages 15 to 80) in which life review techniques are employed to elicit life crises from the participants. Butler believes that these 2 approaches are useful for negotiating a successful old age.

20-4. Butler, R. N. (1980-1981). The life review: An unrecognized bonanza. International Journal of Aging and Human Development, 12, 35-38.

Active listening as a clinical procedure can be helpful to the physician entrusted with the care of older patients. In this way, oral history can play an important role in the evaluation of the older adult. This approach is a humanistic method of evaluation that benefits client and doctor alike.

20-5. Haight, B. K. (1991). Reminiscing: The state of the art as a basis for practice. International Journal of Aging and Human Development, 33, 1-32.

This review essay summarizes the findings of 97 different articles on life review and reminiscence (1960-1990). Only 7 report negative results. Haight recommends that clinical specialists ought to employ reminiscence in their practices. This is an excellent evaluative reference.

20-6. Merriam, S. (1980). The concept and function of reminiscence: A review of the research. The Gerontologist, 20, 604-609.

A precise and commonly agreed upon definition of the notion of reminiscence is elusive. In part, this difficulty arises from a confusion of this notion with others such as memory, and life review. Reminiscence serves as an adaptive mechanism and may help in personality reorganization in later life. This study is a first step toward a theory of reminiscence which will, necessarily, entail more research.

20-7. Molinari, V., & Reichlin, R. E. (1984-1985). Life review reminiscence in the elderly: A review of the literature. International Journal of Aging and Human Development, 20, 81-92.

Since the appearance of Butler's groundbreaking essay on the life review process in older adults, much attention has been paid to this concept in the literature. In this review essay, Molinari and Reichlin review the extant literature to assess what is known and remains to be examined. The process itself is a personalized self-evaluation with intra- and interpersonal elements. The authors of this article state that it is necessary to distinguish the life review from other more common forms of reminiscences. Likewise, a more suitable definition of this process is necessary. Other areas for future research include: (1) longitudinal studies; (2) community-living versus independent living arrangements, and (3) intra- and interpersonal components of the life review.

20-8. Romaniuk, M. (1981). Review: Reminiscence and the second half of life. Experimental Aging Research, 7, 315-337.

This thorough review of the literature on reminiscence is an excellent resource for materials through 1981. Romaniuk determines that the phenomenon of reminiscence is a complex, and incompletely understood process which possesses many variables (content, frequency, form, function, affect and outcome and eliciting stimuli). The author offers suggestions for future research in this area (reminiscence triggers, specific aspects, content, etc.).

20-9. Ryant, C. A. (1981). Comment: Oral history and gerontology. The Gerontologist, 21, 104-105.

Ryant outlines the values (life review, therapeutic effect on the participant) and the dangers (exploitation of older adults, and pseudo-psychology) of oral history which is the audio and/or video recording of interviews with older adults to capture their recollections and reminiscences about earlier periods. A useful list of basic oral history references is included.

20-10. Tarman, V. I. (1988). Autobiography: The negotiation of a lifetime. International Journal of Aging and Human Development, 27, 171-191.

In this review of the literature on reminiscence and life-review studies, Tarman shows that there is a developmental (sequential, unidirectional, qualitative, universal changes), and an interpretive approach (a study of an individual's covert behavior). Tarman then proceeds to review Erving Goffman's dramaturgical sociological perspective and its possible application to these 2 forms of autobiography. The author concludes that in addition to the existing problems associated with reminiscence studies (conflicting and inclusive results), yet another must be noted, namely, the failure to account for the social dimension of reminiscence.

20-11. Thompson, P. (1978). The voice of the past: Oral history. 2nd ed. Oxford: Oxford University Press.

This outstanding resource work constitutes a complete manual for oral history. The topics covered include: (1) history and the community; (2) historians and oral history; (3) achievement of oral history; (4) evidence; (5) memory and the self; (6) exemplary projects; (7) the oral interview; (8) storing the data and its evaluation; and (9) the interpretation of oral history.

20-12. Thornton, S., & Brotchie, J. (1987). Reminiscence: A critical review of the empirical literature. British Journal of Clinical Psychology, 26, 93-111.

In this thorough review of previous empirical studies on reminiscence in the older adult, the authors report variation in the definitions of reminiscence, and procedures for the elicitation of such activity. Thornton and Brotchie conclude from their critical assessment that little evidence exists for reminiscence in older people. Furthermore, the functions of reminiscence are imprecise. Moreover, its therapeutic value is questioned.

21

TELEVISION

21-1. Age stereotyping and television. (1977). Hearing before the Select Committee on Aging. House of Representatives 95th Congress. First session. September 9. Comm. Publication No. 95-109.

This free governmental publication contains the statements of 9 congressional representatives, 8 expert witnesses, and 4 appendices with statements by the staff of the Select Committee on Aging, Herminio Traviesas (National Broadcasting Company), Nicholas Johnson (National Citizens Communications Lobby), and Edward F. Ansello (University of Maryland, College Park, MD). Researchers will find this to be a useful introduction to issues related to the depiction of aging and older adults in television programming.

21-2. Aronoff, C. (1974). Old age in prime time. Journal of Communication, 24, 86-87.

This brief summary of a study of 2,741 television characters during 1969-1971 reveals that older adults of both sexes constitute less than 5% of all characters. Moreover, older people in television tend to be depicted negatively (unsuccessful, unhappy, and evil).

21-3. Atkin, C. K. (1976). Mass media and the aging. In H. J. Oyer, & E. J. Oyer (Eds.), Aging and communication (pp. 99-118). Baltimore, MD: University Park Press.

In this review essay, the author studies 4 basic elements of the mass media and older adults: (1) the depiction of older people in the media; (2) their exposure to the media; (3) their evaluation of the media; and (4) why older persons use the media. Social science and applied research questions that require answers are specified. Finally, future trends and a set of recommendations for future investigations are suggested.

21-4. Barton, R. L., & Schreiber, E. (1978). Media and aging: A critical review of an expanding field of communication research. Central States Speech Journal, 29, 173-186.

In this overview of extant research on media and aging, the author examines 6 major areas: (1) media-use behavior and demographics of older viewers; (2) age-related media content; (3) effect of an older person's use of the media on individual response to aging; (4) societal consequences of the interdependence of the media and aging; (5) structure and function of media organizations as a source of influence on aging; and (6) tactics for media use of aging themes and issues. A set of suggestions of issues for future research is offered. This reference is a good point of departure for the person who wants to know the basic issues of aging and television.

21-5. Batra, G., & Nuessel, F. (1985). The commercial enterprise: The depiction of the elderly in the media. The Gerontologist, 25 (special issue), 75-76.

In this study of 350 different television commercials for a 24-hour period in Boston, MA, 6 variables were examined: (1) age of actor; (2) gender of actor; (3) product category; (4) role status of older adults; (5) competency and vitality of the older person; and (6) manifestations of ageism.

21-6. Beck, K. (1978). Television and the older woman. Television Quarterly, 15, 47-49.

A double standard of aging exists in television. Younger women garner favor and attention because of their sexual appeal. Older women, however, are usually unattractive and possess undesirable personality traits. By comparison, older men are portrayed as appealing, interesting, powerful and socially adept. The author cites several popular television programs from the 1970s to buttress her assertions.

21-7. Bishop, J. M., & Krause, D. R. (1984). Depictions of aging and old age on Saturday morning television. The Gerontologist, 24, 91-94.

106 cartoons broadcast on television on Saturday mornings (7-11:00 a.m.) for 6 weeks (October-November 1981) were coded for 4 elements of content: (1) relative frequency of older characters; (2) quality of their depiction; (3) number of aging themes; and (4) references to age and aging. Instances of older characters and aging were infrequent, yet these few cases were usually negative and stereotypic. The authors argue, however, that this may be sufficient to influence children to accept the common cultural perception of older adults.

21-8. Cassata, M. B., Anderson, P. A., & Skill, T. D. (1980). The older adult in daytime serial drama. Journal of Communication, 30, 48-49.

The data base for this study derived from a 2 week sample (June-July 1978) that covered 13 daytime television serials. Of 365 characters, 58 (15.9%) were judged to be over 55. The authors conclude that older adults portrayed in the sample conveyed a positive image (independence, involvement in work and family, attractiveness).

21-9. Dail, P. W. (1988). Prime-time television portrayals of older adults in the context of family life. The Gerontologist, 28, 700-706.

A total of 3,469 verbal expressions and behaviors evaluated in a sample of 193 characters who portray older adults was examined to determine a family-life context. 5 variables (cognitive ability, physical deportment, health, social situation, and affective expression) were assessed. In general, older adults (over 55) are characterized in a positive fashion. Nevertheless, older women are depicted stereotypically and negatively far more often than older men. Educational and research implications are discussed.

21-10. Davis, R. H. (1971). Television and the older adult. Journal of Broadcasting, 15, 153-159.

A questionnaire was sent to members of the American Association of Retired Persons in Long Beach, California in December, 1969 to determine television usage by older adults. A total of 350 forms were distributed, and 174 were returned. Information sought included: (1) demographic data; (2) television usage and viewing patterns; (3) program preferences; and (4) attitudes and opinions. Results indicated that 74% of the population was over 66, and 28% was over 74. 75% of the respondents indicated that they watched television less than 5 hours per week. Program preferences (in order) were for news, educational programs, and travel.   64.5% of the people surveyed assessed television programming as "satisfactory," while 77.7% denied that television advertising influenced their purchases.

21-11. Davis, R. H. (1980). Television and the aging audience. Los Angeles: The University of Southern California Press.

In this important and excellent introduction to television and aging, the author discusses significant issues related to this medium: (1) the portrayal of older people; (2) the use of television by older adults; (3) media guidelines for the depiction of older characters; (4) how to access the media; and (5) examples of programs about older people from commercial and public television.

21-12. Davis, R. H. (1982). TV and the elderly: A search for values. Media and Values, 19, 8-9.

Television has a number of important functions for older adults. Involvement, companionship, daily time demarcation, and time structure. This medium plays an important role in the life of the older adult. Because of their greater use of television, older adults may be affected adversely by its content (seeing the world as hostile, and reduced self-esteem).

21-13. Davis, R. H. (1984). TV's boycott of old age. Aging, 346, 12-17.

Television programming is aimed at the 18 to 55 year old market because this demographic sector represents the target audience of its commercial sponsors. One result of this situation is television's tendency to ignore older adults. When older people and aging are depicted on television, distortion and ageism frequently exist. Davis exhorts the reader to watch programming about aging as one means of encouraging the creation of similar efforts.

21-14. Davis, R. H., & Davis, J. A. (1985). TV's image of the elderly: A practical guide for change. Lexington, MA: Lexington Books.

This exhaustive and valuable study explores virtually all aspects of television and its relationship to older adults. Part I ("Television and the Aging Audience") contains 6 chapters (the aging society, the medium itself, the image of old age, the older adults audience, the older viewer, and the related broadcast technologies and the older viewer.) Part II ("Helping Shape Television Coverage") features 5 more chapters on various important themes (programming of age-oriented topics, securing your own television show, production of a television show, guest appearances, advocacy of aging rights). 4 appendices

("You and Television," "Sample Scripts," "Topics," "Glossary"), and a useful index complement this book.

21-15. Diamond, E. (1980, February). Ah Youth! Ah Television! American Film, 16, 74.

In this "point of view" essay, Diamond comments upon the presence of older people on television. In his view, network executives prefer attractive, authoritative, and objective people to create a homogenized, and idealized image of reality.

21-16. Downing, M. (1974). Heroine of the daytime serial. Journal of Communication, 24, 130-137.

In this examination of 20 episodes each of 15 daytime television serials for the period June-August 1973 (N = 300), the author and 5 assistants monitored the programs to ascertain the role and function of women. Of 256 characters, 129 were female. The author found that aging affected women negatively through a loss of occupational status. Moreover, older women are generally not cast in roles in daytime serials because young women are the norm in this time slot.

21-17. Elliott, J. C. (1982). Images of older adult characters on daytime television serial drama (Doctoral dissertation, Teachers College, Columbia University, 1981). Dissertation Abstracts International, 43, 1736A-1737A.

During the period July-November 1979, 13 daytime television serials dramas (260 total episodes) were evaluated by the author and 4 additional monitors to ascertain the images of older adults. Of 58 characters, 35 were male and 23 female which represented 8% of all of the characters with speaking parts in the programs surveyed. Stereotypic old age was not depicted in these serials.

21-18. Elliott, J. C. (1984). The daytime television drama portrayal of older adults. The Gerontologist, 24, 628-633.

The data for this study is based on a scrutiny of 13 daytime (11:30 a.m. to 4:30 p.m.) television serial dramas broadcast from July 27 to November 9, 1979. Variables such as gender, verbal and affective behavior, and role were recorded. Results showed that 8% of the characters were older adults. These characters generally defied stereotypic myths. Men, however, appeared more often (2:1 ratio) than women in minor roles. Likewise, men were depicted in more diverse roles.

21-19. Elliott, J. (1986). Review of TV's image of the elderly: A practical guide for change by R. H. Davis, and J. A. Davis. The Gerontologist, 26, 222.

Elliott provides a factual account of the contents of the volume under review. The reviewer notes that the second part of the book is particularly good since it is in this section that the authors provide a blueprint for creating a television show for older adults. The use of this electronic medium as a tool for advocacy will reach the largest audience.

21-20. Francher, J. S. (1973). "It's the Pepsi generation . . .": Accelerated aging and the television commercial. International Journal of Aging and Human Development, 4, 245-255.

In an empirical analysis of 100 randomly selected television commercials, type of product, characters, tone, target group, scene, and implied promise were examined. The author refers to a "youth complex" (emphasis on youthfulness, vigorous activity, and sensory gratification) dominant in many commercials. The author speculates that such idealized youth-oriented messages may have a culturally-disenfranchising effect on older adults' self-esteem.

21-21. Gerbner, G., Gross, L., Signorielli, N., & Morgan, M. (1980). Aging with television: Images on television drama and conceptions of social reality. Journal of Communication, 30, 37-47.

The data base for this study included programming on the 3 major networks broadcast during a single week of prime time (8-11 p.m. EST), and weekend daytime (8 a.m. to 2 p.m. Saturday and Sunday) during the years 1969-1978, and for a week each in spring of 1975 and 1976. The information gathered included sex, race, class, age, role-type, and program type.   Under-representation of older adults was pronounced in this survey since older adults comprise 11% of the U.S. population but only 2.3% of the television characters. In the case of weekend daytime characters, even fewer older people are present (1.4%). Depiction of character traits depends upon age. Evil increases with age for men and women. Success, on the other hand, increases with age for men, but decreases as women grow older. In a test constructed by the authors, a correlation between amount of television watched and negative perception of older people emerged.

21-22. Greenberg, B. S., Korzenny, F., & Atkin, C. K. (1979). The portrayal of the aging: Trends on commercial television. Research on Aging, 1, 319-334.

The sample for this study included a single episode of regularly scheduled prime time programs 8-11 p.m. M-F, and 8 a.m. to 12:30 p.m. Saturday) for the fall seasons of 1975, 1976, and 1977. Results revealed that only 3% of the characters in the 64 and older group appeared in the sample. Likewise, there were more older male characters than female characters. The authors, however, do not believe that older people are depicted in an overwhelmingly negative way. Finally, it is suggested that it would be better to ascertain who the audience judges to be old rather than relying on simple chronological categorizations.

21-23. Harris, A. J., & Feinberg, J. F. (1977). Television and aging: Is what you see what you get? The Gerontologist, 17, 464-468.

The sampling for this study derived from a 6-week period (October-November 1976) for time slots (8 a.m.-noon, noon-4 p.m., 4 p.m.-8 p.m., and 8 p.m.-midnight). The authors found that the demographic representation of older adults reflected closely actual population statistics. Character development of older people, however, was poor. Moreover, older women fared worse than men in their depiction. The authors speculate on the impact of television in shaping popular attitudes about older people.

21-24. Hiemstra, R., Goodman, M., Middlemiss, M. A., Vosco, R., & Ziegler, N. (1983). How older persons are portrayed in television advertising: Implications for educators. Educational Gerontology, 9, 111-122.

A scrutiny of 136 randomly selected television commercials (summer of 1981) were reviewed by using the method of content analysis. Results indicated a dearth of older people in such advertising. Specific findings included the following: (1) 11 of 358 people were rated to be over 60; (2) 41 of 358 were judged to be over 50; (3) 6 of 130 main characters in commercials were considered to be over 60; (4) 66% of the older people were male; and (5) no older characters were African-American.

21-25. Holtzman, J. M., & Akiyama, H. (1985). What children see: The aged on television in Japan and the United States. The Gerontologist, 25, 62-68.

4 episodes each of the top 10 programs in Japan and the United States were recorded in 1982. Variables analyzed by recorders included age, gender, role status, health, socio-economic group. It was determined that older characters with speaking roles appeared more frequently in U.S. programming (9.4%) than in the Japanese programs (4%). Moreover, older adults appeared a total of 3 hours, 27 minutes, 18 seconds in the U.S. sample versus 1 hour, 37 minutes,

32 seconds in Japanese programs. Finally, older people were depicted in a more positive fashion in the U.S. sample.

21-26. Kubey, R. W. (1980). Television and aging: Past, present, and future. The Gerontologist, 20, 16-35.

In this review essay, the author examines in detail 4 major issues: (1) viewing practices of older adults; (2) the depiction of older adults in television programming; (3) the effect of television on older viewers; and (4) current and future gerontologically-significant issues. This excellent article is one of the most thorough overviews of television's relation to older adults available.

21-27. Larson, R. F. (1976). Images of aging: Producer's viewpoint. The Gerontologist, 16, 368-370.

The author, a television producer for a station in Hershey, PA, comments on a production entitled "images of aging" funded by the Corporation for Public Broadcasting. Larson wanted this series to point out that old people are, in fact, people like anyone else. Public and critical response to the programs was both positive, and broadbased.

21-28. Mundorf, N., & Brownell, W. (1990). Media preferences of older and younger adults. The Gerontologist, 30, 685-691.

In this study, the use of media by older and younger adults are compared. Older adults report a higher level of television viewing than their younger cohorts. Viewing patterns were found to be more similar than different. Nevertheless, some differences were encountered such as age and gender preferences for characters and reasons for viewing. Finally, print media (magazines) preferences were pronounced because of demographic targeting.

21-29. Northcott, H. C. (1975). Too old, too young--age in the world of television. The Gerontologist, 15, 184-186.

In this empirical analysis of the content of television programming (41 shows for a total of 35 hours) for 1 week in February of 1974 (7 to 10 p.m.). Of 464 roles portrayed, only 1.5% appeared to be over 64 years old. Stereotypical depiction of older adults was not a pervasive feature.

21-30. Passuth, P. M., & Cook, F. L. (1985). Effects of television viewing on knowledge about older adults: A critical reexamination. The Gerontologist, 25, 69-77.

In this study, the authors sought to determine the effect of television viewing on attitudes toward and knowledge about older adults. The results indicated that no overall relationship exists between television viewing habits and attitudes and knowledge about older adults. The authors did find that television viewing did affect younger adults' knowledge of older people.

21-31. Petersen, M. (1973). The visibility and image of old people on television. Journalism Quarterly, 50, 569-573.

30 half-hour programs in the 8 to 11 p.m. slot formed the data base for this study of older adults in the media. In comparison to the demographics, older people were over-represented (12.96%) in the sample, although women were significantly absent (1.21%). In general, older people are portrayed favorably.

21-32. Rubin, A. M. (1982). Directions in television and aging research. Journal of Broadcasting, 26, 537-551.

In this review article on television and the aging, the author reviews 3 themes: (1) depiction of older adults on television; (2) television behaviors; and (3) television functions. The author also raises several methodological issues about extant studies, e.g., appropriate definition of older adult, the heterogeneity of the older population, issues of validity and reliability, and univariate statistical practices. Worthwhile suggestions for future research are offered.

21-33. Schalinkse, T. F. (1968). The role of television in the life of the aged person (Doctoral dissertation, The Ohio State University, 1968). Dissertation Abstracts, 9, 989A-990A.

Interviews with 32 women and 18 men who live in age-segregated housing provided the data for this study. Among the findings of this study are the following: (1) television is used extensively by older people even though the programming is youth-oriented; (2) television stations ought to include older people as a part of their programming, especially to fulfill public service commitments; and (3) television demonstrates great potential for satisfying the needs of older people.

21-34. Schramm, W. (1968). Aging and mass communication. In R. W. Riley, J. W. Riley, & M. E. Johnson (Eds.), Aging and society, volume two: Aging and the professions (pp. 352-375). New York: Russell Sage Foundation.

In this review essay, the author notes the failure of the mass media (newspapers, magazines, radio, and television) to address the important issue of America's aging population. In addition, Schramm analyzes the age of the mass media consumers. Third, the use of the media by older adults is examined. Finally, suggestions for strategies to assist older consumers are made.

21-35. Serock, K. E. (1980). An analysis of the portrayal of the elderly in television commercials viewed by children (Doctoral dissertation, University of Maryland, 1979). Dissertation Abstracts International, 40, 3756A-3757A.

During a 10 week period (January to April 1978), half hour time slots were randomly selected for the periods of 8:00 to 10:00 p.m. weeknights, and 8:00 a.m. to 12:00 p.m. Saturdays. From a total of 270 commercials on weeknights, 54 older persons were depicted. Likewise, from a total of 134 commercials on Saturdays, 18 older people were portrayed. Results indicated the following facts: (1) older people were under-represented and more older males than females appeared by a ratio of 2:1; (2) few minorities were represented (only 2 older blacks appeared); (3) weeknight appearances of older people on commercials depicted real people in a serious format while on Saturday mornings, older people were animated cartoon characters cast in a humorous situation; (4) commercials viewed by children depicted older women in domestic contexts, and older men in professional roles; and (5) older people were shown to have a high degree of autonomy compared to children. In general, the depiction of older people was inaccurate and unrealistic.

21-36. Turow, J. (1978). Casting for TV parts: The anatomy of social types. Journal of Communication, 28, 18-24.

In a study designed to determine character selection for television, the author recorded age, sex, ethnicity, and physical qualities. The data base derived from interviews with 5 writers, 9 producers, 3 directors, 15 casting directors, and 5 talent agents. While the number of older people had increased on television, the roles for older men far outnumbered those for older women.

21-37. Wright, K. D. (1973). Mass media and the elderly: Creating public awareness. Perspectives on Aging, 2, 2-4.

Tennessee developed a federally-funded media-based education program including 125 radio and 21 television stations to provide the public with information about older adults in the areas of health, income, transportation, housing, living situations, and location. The state has continued to fund some programs after the cessation of federal funding. The residents of the state are now more informed about these issues.

AUTHOR INDEX

SUBJECT INDEX

About the Author

Frank Nuessel is Professor of Modern Languages at the University of Louisville. His broad research interests include humanistic studies of aging, Hispanic linguistics, and Italian studies. He has published numerous articles in journals such as *Hispanic Linguistics* and the *Journal of Literary Semantics*, and has authored several books, including *The Study of Names: A Guide to the Principles and Topics* (Greenwood Press, 1992).